LYCIA

CONTENTS

LYCIA

Yayınlayan ve Dağıtan :
TEN TURİZM PAZ. LTD.
Kışla Mahallesi 54. Sokak No. 11/A, Antalya-TURKEY
Tel : (+90.242) 248 93 67 Fax : (+90.242) 248 93 68
www.tenturizm.com • e-mail : ten@tenturizm.com
Text : Kemal Hakkı Tor
Photographs : Ahmet Bedel-Pınar Dal-Süleyman Bedel
K.Hakkı Tor ve Net Yayıncılık AŞ Arşivi
Layout : Avni Alan
Printed in Turkey by : Bilnet Matbaacılık Biltur Basım Yayın ve Hizmet A.Ş.

ISBN 978-9944-226-07-3

Page 34 ➡

Page 98 ➡

Page 146 ➡   Page 170 ➡

WELCOME TO LYCIA

Welcome to the mystical and magnificient Lycian region, where the torrent of civilizations overflow through the tunnel of time, gliding down from the inaccessible summits of wild Taurus Mountains, embracing the foamy, dark blue waters of the Mediterranean. Although we are fully aware that words and volumes of books will fail us in our attempts to define this region, crowned with natural and historical treasures, we shall do our utmost, with traditional mediterranean hospitality, to assist you in your extraordinary venture into this bewitching Land. How lucky for us if we can shed a shred of light on your route...

Lycian house type tombs.

Lycia History

George E. Bean, who has compiled various documents on the establishment and history of the Lycian region, furnishes the following details:

"Lycia may be roughly defined as the country lying south of a line drawn from Koycegiz to Antalya. Its boundary in the west is Akdag, the ancient Massieytus and in the east Bey Dağı, the ancient Solyma, both over 10.000 feet high. To the west of Akdağ is the valley of Xanthus, with beyond it the minor range of Cragus and Anticragus; to the east of Bey Dağı, is the valley of the Alakır (ancient name uncertain), with beyond it the minor range of Tahtalı Dağ. These rivers are the largest in the country; the even longer Dalaman Çayı to the northwest is not genuinely in Lycia. The northern part of the country consists of a comparatively level plateau consistently over 3.000 feet above the sea.

"So mountainous a land was bound to be thinly and unevenly inhabited; the total population in antiquity has been estimated at a mere 200.000. All the chief cities are on the coast or in the Xanthus valley; this latter was the true heart of Lycia. In summer the day temperature is regularly over 90° F; the modern in-

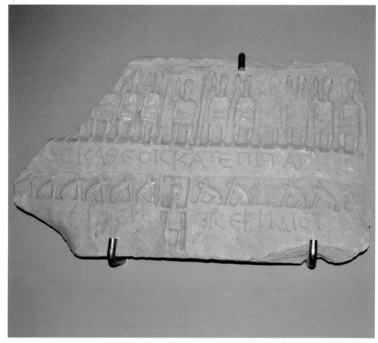

Lycian Dedicatory Steles (Antalya Museum).

habitants, unless they have business to detain them, leave their villages when the crops arein in June and make their way to the high ground to the north, and there is reason to believe that the ancients did the same.

Between may and mid-September rainfall is scanty; in the central region there is no running water and the people are dependent on wells, it,is not uncommon for these to dry up before the time comes for the summer migration. Altogether a hard land, and it had a hardy folk.

"Among the various races of Anatolia, the Lycians always held a distinctive place. Locked away in their mountainous country, they had a fierce love of freedom and independence, and resisted strongly all attempts at outside domination; they were the last in

Asia Minor to be incorporated as a province in the Roman Empire. They had a language of their own which is still imperfectly understood, written in characters many of which are peculiar to it. They had an instinct for union and federation, and formed a Lycian nation when elsewhere the Greek world was made up of individual city-states perpetually at enmity with one another. They had customs of their own and a style of funerary architecture which is quite unique.

"Where did they come from, and when? The Greek tradition is recorded by Herodotus, who says they came originally from Crete; when Minos and his brother Sarpedon quarrelled for the power, Minos was victorious and Sarpedon with his followers crossed to Asia and settled in Lycia, which was then called Milyas, driving out the Solymi who were in occupation. For a time they kept their name of Termilae (which is still used by their neighbours), but when Lycus, son of Pandion king of Athens, expelled by his brother Aegeus, came to join Sarpedon, they took from him their name of Lycians. The traditional date for Pandion

as recorded by the Parian Marble is the early thirteenth century, whereas Minos and Sarpedon are placed in the latter half of the fifteenth century. These dates are of course quite unreliable, and the chronology is further confused by a later Minos in the time of Lycus and Aegeus and a later Sarpedon in the time of the Trojan war (late thirteenth century).

"Chronologically much surer ground is afforded by the Hittite records, which refer a number of times to a nation of the Lukka, who can be no other than the Lycians. We learn that the Lukka lands were conquered by the Hittites in the reign of Suppiluliumas in the mid-fourteenth century, tough they were not securely held but were often in rebellion.

Further evidence comes from the tablets found at Tel-el-Amarna in Egypt, where certain Lukki are mentioned among a group of sea-raiders about the same time. For the location of the Lukka lands the indications are mostly vague; they seem to have been close neighbours of the Arzawa some-where to the west or south-west of the Hittite capital Hattusas. This, combined with the description of them as sea-raiders, would naturally place them in Caria and/or Lycia. There is, howev-er, one more precise piece of evidence. The records mention a city of Dalawa in the Lukka Lands; if, as seems vir-tually certain, this is the same as the Lycian Tlawa, that is Tlos, in the Xanthos Valley, the location of the Lukka in Lycia in the fourteenth cen-tury is established. Furthermore, Dalawa is associated in the records with the city of Hinduwa, which is likely to be identical with the classi-cal Candyba.

"There seems accordingly nothing to prevent us from accepting the set-tlement of Lycia, perhaps towards 1400 B.C., by Cretans under Sarpedon. According to the historian Ephorus they came first to Caria, where they founded the city of Miletus, calling it after the Cretan city of the same name. Another tradition asserted that the Carian city of Idrias, later Straton-

Lycian Dedicatory Steles.

iceia, was the first city founded by the Lycians; if this has any historical ba-sis, it will mark the passage of the Ly-cians southward from Miletus to their eventual home. Herodotus story of the name Lycian being taken from the Athenian Lycus, improbable in itself,

Child Sarcophagus tombs (Antalya Museum).

is obviously to be rejected.

"Not so his assertion that the Lycians were originally called Termilae. Not only is this repeated by other ancient writers, but it is strikingly confirmed by the incriptions in the native language, which refer to them always as TRMMILI, never as Lycians The Greek inscriptions, on the contrary, never use the name Termilae; even the Xanthian Obelisk, about 400 B.C., in its Greek portion speaks of Lycians. The Lycian inscriptions date to the late fifth and fourth centuries, or barely later than Herodotus' time. Not merely the neighbours, therefore, but the Lycians themselves continued to use the name Termilae. It is not, of course, rare for a people to call themselves by a name different from that used by others; the modern Greeks and Germans are obvious examples; nevertheless, it is possible that the Termilae are to be distinguished, as later incomers, from the Lukka or Lycians. If so, the language of the inscriptions should more properly be called Termilie.

"The great majority of the texts consists of epitaphs; the principal exceptions are the Xanthian Obelisk, which contains a good deal of historical and other matter, and a new trilingual text from the Letoum referring to the institution of a religious cult. Heredotus observes that the Lycian customs are partly Cretan, partly Carian; they have, however, he says, one custom which is peuliar to them and unique among mankind : They reckon their lineage not by the father's but by the mother's side. Ask a Lycian who

Corner Blok With Relief - Xanthos.

Dressed Women Statue-Arykanda.

he is and he will name his mother and his mother's mothers. Moreover, the children of a female citizen, even from a slave, are reckoned legitimate, whereas those of a male citizen from a foreigner or a concubine are illegitimate".

The earliest appearance of the Lycians in Greek literature is in Homer's Iliad, where they fight as allies of the Trojans, coming 'from distant Lycia and eddying Xanthus'; their Commanders Sarpedon and Glaucus play a not undistinguished part among minor heroes. Homer is now generally agreed to have composed towards 700 B.C.; by the sixth century the Lydian kings had conquered the whole of Asia Minor west of the river Halys with the exception of the Lycians and the Cilicians. The last king of Lydia, Croesus, fell to the Persians in 546 B.C., and his

Xanthos Obelisk inscription detail0

kingdom passed to them. The Persians were not willing to leave the Lycians in freedom, and sent an army under their general Harpagus to subdue them; after a desperate resistance the Lycians submitted to superior force. Persian rule was mild, requiring little more than the payment of tribute, and the country was left to be governed by its own dynasts; by the end of the century these were striking silver coins in their own names..

In 480 B.C., when Xerxes assembled his huge force for the conquest of Greece, the Lycians contributed fifty ships to his fleet; the men, says Herodotus, wore breast plates and greaves, with bows of cornel wood, unwinged arrows of reed, javelins, goat-skins over their shoulders, and feathered hats on their heads, also daggers and scimitars. Of their exploits in the war we

Xanthos Obelisk inscription.

Caunos-Dalyan.

hear nothing. When the Peloponnesian War ended in 404 with the complete defeat of Athens by Sparta, the Delian Confederacy ceased to exist. Sparta took over, but had not the qualitiez for managing an overseas empire, and Lycia fell back under Persian domination. During all this time the Lycian dynasts continued to issue their silver coinage. In the early fourth century the Persian satrap of Caria was Mausolus, an energetic and ambitious man who took advantage of the slack Persian rule to make himself in effect an independent despot; in addition to the whole of Caria he extended his claims to Lycia also. The Lycians resisted under their dynast Pericles; only Phaselis, still not a true Lycian city, accepter Mausolus, and even concluded a treaty with him. Pericles, treating Phaselis as an enemy, submitted her to a blockade.

Any pretensions of Mausolus' successors to control of Lycia ended with the arrival of Alexander in 333. After the reduction of Halicarnassus, Alexander proceeded to Lycia, where he made a treaty with Telmessus, then, crossing the Xanthus, received the surrender of Pinara, Xanthus, and some thirty minor cities. Phaselis showed herself especially friendly; she offered him her submission together with a golden crown, and Alexander stayed some time in the city, incidentally lending her his troops to subdue some troublesome neighhours. He then moved on into Pamphylia.

Lycian Dedicatory Steles.

Kaya Village.

After Alexander's death Lycia came into the power of his general Ptolemy, who had established himself as king of Egypt. Ptolemaic control continued for about a hundred years, and it was during this period that the Lycian Language died out and was replaced by Greek; the rule of the dynasts had come to an end with Pericles and the cities adopted Greek constitutions.

In 197 B.C. the country was taken from the Ptolemies by Antiochus 111., king of Syria; Phaselis, Limyra, Andriace, Patara, and Xanthus are specially mentioned as having been captured by him. He was shortly afterwards defeated by the Romans at the battle of Magnesia; in the settlement which followed in 189 Lycia, with the exception of Telmessus, was given to the Rhodians, who had supported Rome. The Lycians, intolerant as ever of foreign domination, resisted bitterly, claiming that they had been given to Rhodes not as subjects but as allies; the Rhodians claimed complete suzerainty, and for ten years there was fierce fighting. In 177 the Lycians, no longer able to hold out, sent an embassy to Rome to complain of the harshness of Rhodian rule. Roman relations with Rhodes had by this time cooled, and the Senate gave the Lycians a favourable reply, to the effect that they were supposed to be merely friends and allies of the Rhodians. Encouraged by this, the Lycians took up arms again, and hostilities continued for another six years, but by 171 the Lycians were again exhausted. In 167, however, the Senate decided to put an end to Rhodian control of Caria and Lycia and declared these countries free. Only one result of the Rhodian rule in Lycia was of any permanence : Phaselis, a Rhodian colony by origin, was at last included in Lycia with her western neighbours.

Some time in the second century, perhaps near the beginning, two men, Lysanias and Eudemus, seized control of the city of Xanthus, carried out executions, and attempted to set up a tyranny. A campaign of the League foces was needed to supress them and restore the situation. Shortly afterwards Eudemus made a second attempt at Tlos, and again the League forces had to be called in. It is evident that at the time of these events the Lycian League was in full vigour and ready to act in the defence of liberty.

In the long period of freedom after 167 B.C. the Lycian League came into prominence. It was not a new phenomenon; the Lycians had always an instinct for union and collaboration; and even under the dynasts of the fourth century the Lycian inscriptions refer repeatedly to the payment of fines to the 'Federal Treasurer of The Termilae'. Concerning this early federation we have no precise information.

Xanthos South Gate.

most important cities have three votes each, the less important two, and the others one. Taxes and other public burdens are allocated in these proportions to the various cities. At the congress a Lyciarchis is chosen, then the other

Of the later League, on the other hand, we have a detailed account by Strabo, supplemented by what we learn from the inscriptions. Strabo says there are twenty-three cities possessing the vote; they 'come together from each city' to a federal congress at a city chosen for the occasion; the League officials and panels of judges; minor magistrates and jurors in the federal courts are elected from each city proportional to its voting power. Formerly the congress decided questions of war, peace and alliance, but now these decisions, save in special cases, naturally rest rather with Romans.

Ships Island-Fethiye.

This account is in general well substantiated by our other information; it is, however, unsatisfactory in one respect, the nature of the 'congress'. The inscriptions, which are of course unassailable evidence, make no mention of a 'congress', but rather of two bodies, a Council and an Assembly, the latter generally styled electoral. From his account of its functions it seems Strabo's 'congress' must be the Assembly, and that he errs in omitting the Council. For the composition of the congress his words 'they come together from the cities' are certainly vague, and here again the inscriptions help to fill in the picture. They make it clear that the Assembly was not, as it normally was in a Greek city, a primary assembly of the whole body of the citizens, but consist-

Corner Blok With Relief - Xanthos (Antyalya Museum).

Sarcophagus Inscription – Sidyma.

ed of a limited number of delegates from the individual cities, determined in each case by the city's voting power. This system of representative government, with privileges and obligations in direct ratio to the city's classification, is the outstanding feature of the Lycian League.

Strabo's figure of twenty-three voting cities is astonishingly low. He had his information from Artemidorus, who wrote about 100 B.C., and it presumably refers to the situation at that time. Pliny, in the first century A.D., says there were formerly seventy cities in Lycia, but only thirty-six in his time .

After the grant of freedom in 167 B.C. we hear little of Lycian affairs until the first Mithridatic war; the forma-

tion of the Roman province of Asia in 129 left Lycia untouched. In 88 the Pontic king Mithridates VI attacked and overran western Asia Minor; Roman administration had been so unsatisfactory that most places welcomed him as a liberator, but Lycia was among the few that resisted. Mithridates sent his officers to subdue it, and the Lycians had much to endure; the king himself made only one brief appeance at Patara, and Lycia was not effectively occupied. The war ended in 84 with the king's defeat by Sulla, and in the subsequent settlement the Romans showed their appreciation of the Lycian's loyalty by confirming their freedom and enlarging their territory by the addition of the three cities of Bubon, Balbura, and Oenoanda.

During the Roman civil wars of the first century B.C. the Lycians had again to suffer from the depredations of Brutus and Cassius, the 'tyrannicides' responsible for the murder of Julius Caesar in 44. The Lycian reluctance to contribute to Brutus resources resulted in the capture and destruction of Xanthos. Upon their defeat at Philippi in 42 by Anthony and Octavian, Anthony received the East as his share of the Roman world, and he too confirmed the freedom of Lycia, which thus remained as the only part of Asia Minor not incorporated in the Roman sphere of power. This state of affeirs came at last to an end in A.D. 43, when Claudius joined Lycia with Pamphylia as a Roman province. This was not, however, quite the last of Lycian freedom, which was given back for a short while by Nero (A.D. 69 - 79.) until vespasian finally restored the composite province on a lasting basis.

Even under the Empire the Lycian League Continued to function. Ques-

Monumental tombs of the king Perikles of Lycia (Heroo) - Limyra (Antalya Museum).

tions of war and peace, as Strabo observes, were naturally left to the Romans, but internal affairs, justice, and security, were still controlled by the League officials, who continued to be regularly appointed. The country was prosperous, money was plentiful, and huge fortunes could be amassed by privete citizens; some of these, like Jason of Cyaneae and Opramoas of Rhodiapolis, made lavish gifts of money not only to their own cities, but also to many others in Lycia.

At the same time most of the cities remained small; a total population of 200.000 gives an average of only some 5.00 for each city.

Although joined in a single province, Lycia and Pamphylia were an ill-assorted pair; the nature of the two countries and the character of the inhabitants were quite unlike. They naturally shared a Roman governor, but in practice each functioned separate-ly. Each had its own magistrades headed by a Lyciarch or Pamphyliarch and managed its affairs with little or no regard for the other. Not that this mattered; the composite province continued quite happily until it was finally split up by Diocletian in the early fourth century. At this time too the boundary of Lycia was extended to the north-west to include the Carian city of Caunus; Calynda had been added to the province at the time of its formation.

Nowhere in Anatolia is there a better opportunity to appreciate the native culture than in Lycia. Here as elsewhere the early buildings have been overlaid by those of the Hellenistic and especially the Roman periods; but the Lycian tombs, for which the country is famous, are in many cases earlier than the time of Alexander, and are morever frequently adorned with sculptures. Many are still in excellent preservation.

Sarcophagus of the champion- Patara (Antalya Museum).

The early tombs fall into four distinct classes, generally called pillar-tombs, temple-tombs, house-tombs, and sarcophagi. The pillar-tombs are usually reckoned to be the earliest and are peculiar to Lycia. They consist of a rectangular pillar set on a base, with a grave-chamber at the top

surmounted by a wide cap-stone. This is the least common type and seems to be confined to the western part of the country. The temple-tombs are not specifically Lycian, and differ little from those of Caunus and other parts of Anatolia. They have simply the facade of a temple, with two columns in antis, usually in the Ionic order, an epistyle, and a pediment. A porch leads through by a door to the grave-chamber, a plain room with stone benches on which the dear were laid. The house-tombs are in imitation of wooden houses, in one, two or occasionally three storeys; the square beam-ends are left projecting. There is normally a row of round or square beam-ends above the door; later these develop into a dentil frieze. There is sometimes, but not always, a pediment above and in a few cases, this has the shape of a pointed ('Gothic') arch. The interior is sim-

Tomb chamber with the lion relief-Arycanda.

Mask relief.

Patara artery.

ilar to that of the temple -tombs. Sarcophagi are of course one of the commonest forms of tomb all over the world, but the early Lycian type is distinctive. It is generally remarkable for its height and is in three parts, a base, a grave-chamber, and a crested 'Gothic' lid. The base is commonly used as a second grave-chamber (hyposorion), destined for the owner's slaves or de-

Tlos stone relief.

pendants. On pillar-tombs sculpture is confined, when it occurs at all, to the sides of the grave - chamber at the top; the well-known example is the 'Harpy Tomb' at Xanthus.

House - tombs are often decorated with reliefs on the walls, in the pediment and sometimes on the adjoining rocks; the most famous case is the istic types there are in Lycia many other forms of tomb, some very striking.

Splendid tombs, both rock-cut and of masonry, are found in most parts of Asia Minor, though nowhere in such abundance as in Lycia. Veneration for ancestors, amounting even to ancestor-worship, was almost universal

Lycian dead ashes stored container (Antalya Museum).

'Painted Tomb' at Myra. Sarcophagi too are very frequently ornamented with reliefs, mostly on the sides and crest of the lid, but also in some cases on the grave-chamber itself. In the Roman period the sarcophagi become much smaller and simpler and the lid is rounded though still with a crest. In addition to these four character-

in the ancient world. At Olympus in eastern Lycia two tombs carry letter-oracles where the response is conceived as given by the ancestor, and in general much care was taken for the preservation of the tomb from damage or misuse. Epitaths commonly end with the imprecation of a curse and/or a pecuniary fine for violation, and in Lycia we sometimes find the tomb under the care of a body called the mindis (MINTI in Lycian), apparently a committee of relatives charged with its protection. Fines for violation were in general payable to the city treasury, or in Roman times to the Imperial chest, the amount being fixed by the owner; he would pay a certain percentage of the chosen sum to the city officials, who would be responsible for convicting the offender and collecting the fine. In the Lycian inscriptions of the fourth century, however, we find a different system in use. The owner makes over the tomb to the mindis, who assume responsibility for its care; for this privilege he pays a modest fee, normally three starters. Later, in the Greek inscriptions, much less is heard of the

mindis; the city takes over, and by Roman times the system familiar elsewhere was in normal operation in Lycia also".

Xanthos Harpy monument and tower sarcophagus.

DALYAN-CAUNOS

+36° 49′52,45′′ • +28° 38′ 22,80′′

One of the places you may visit on the way from Muğla to Fethiye is Dalyan. This small town lies along the highway and after Ortaca is situated on the long canal by which the Köyceğiz lake is connected to the sea. The weir for fishing, where large grey mullets and fish-roe are produced, give the place its name, and this is a major source of income for the in habitants in the province. Dalyan separates the drinkable water of the Köyceğiz lake from the salty sea by a miles-long beach and boasts of the existence of the antique city of CAUNOS. Thus it is a prominent natural and historical site. The exact date of establishment of the city is not definite. However, the mythology regarding how Caunos, son of the King of Miletos, set up the city in 3.000 B.C. runs as follows: "The king of Milletos has twins: a girl named Byblis and a boy called Caunos. Byblis loves her brother so much that she cannot stop fondling him. Well aware that such feelings are unnatural, she writes a letter to Caunos, revealing that her devotion to him exceeds a fraternal affection. Upon reading this letter, Caunos is disgusted and leaves Miletos and sets off to the open sea in order to get away from this sickening love and to avoid facing Byblis again. He establishes the city of Caunos on the Lycian-Carian border. Byblis cannot bear to be parted from him and, losing all hope of finding Caunos, jumps off the rocks in a suicidal attempt. Just then the gods take pity on her and turn her into a stream. Since then, all hopeless love affairs all over the world are called LOVE OF

İstuzu Beach.

General Panorama of Dalyan.

CAUNOS". This antique city, purported to be established by the legendary son of the king, appears both as a Lycian and a Carrian settlement in the course of history. On the basis of language, beliefs, clothing and way of life, however, it has unique national character. Caunos was a center for production of figs, salt and salted fish as well as a major commercial harbour in its time. For a while it was an independent city. Later on, like all its neighbours, it fell under the domination of Persians, Alexander the Great, Roman and Byzantian Empire. Towards the end of the Byzantine rule, the sea around the city and the harbour were covered with sand and as it was cut off from the shore, its prominence as a port was diminished. The province was a major city during the rule of Menteşeoğulları in 1291 and of the Ottoman Empire in 1424. The first point of interest as one enters the antique city is the city walls which must have been built in the 5 th century B.C. The acropolis built on a steep hill to the east of the city and the Caunos antique theater on the west are in pretty good shape. In the city there are also a Roman bath, paloestra, some remains of temples and three Christian churches. On the steep rocks along the canal on the beach there is an imperial tomb, which is similar to Lycian rock tombs built in the fourth century B.C. This is left unfinished supposedly due to the invasion of Alexander the Great.

Recently Dalyan became a source of a world-wide interest for

Tombs of Caunos.

Caunos Theater.

another reason: The last generation of the seatortoises that have existed on earth for 95 million years and might well be called "living history" are now struggling to survive along the Dalyan shores. Their ancestors have adopted to life-in-water years before dinasours existed, and the metamorphosis of the huge land tortoises continued millions of years. Although the ancestor on land have long become extinct, the sea tortoises have somehow managed to survive until now. There are only two kinds of these tortoises living in the seas around our country out of the seven species in existence all around the

Caunos city ruins.

Place covered with rushes in Dalyan.

world. Green Tortoise (Chelonia mydas) It is brown, has a shell, and is almost 3.3 feet long and weighs about 300 pounds. It feeds on sea plants growing in shallow water and the green plants give colour to its body fat, so it is called green tortoise. This is the only sea animal that feeds on sea weeds and it is decreasing in number II. Common Sea Tortoise (Caretta Caretta) its weight is around 60-180 kgs. and it feeds on crabs and similar sea animals. This common sea tortoise hunting near the rocks and corals can easily be distinguished by its thick head and neck. Since it cannot pull its head into its shell like the land tortoises, its head and fins are defenceless. The baby tortoises have plenty of enemies during the early stages of their lives. A recent study has shown that out of 1.000 tortoises just coming out of their eggs only 1-2 can reach maturity. As a fully groun tortoise, due to its size and speed, the tortoise can avoid its enemies. It is a shame that, like many other species, sea tortoises face the danger of extinction due to exploitation, for the sake of tourism, of their natural reproduction areas, as well as haphazard hunting in our days. Dalyan beach has recently been declared a natural reservation area and, as such, further construction is prohibited.

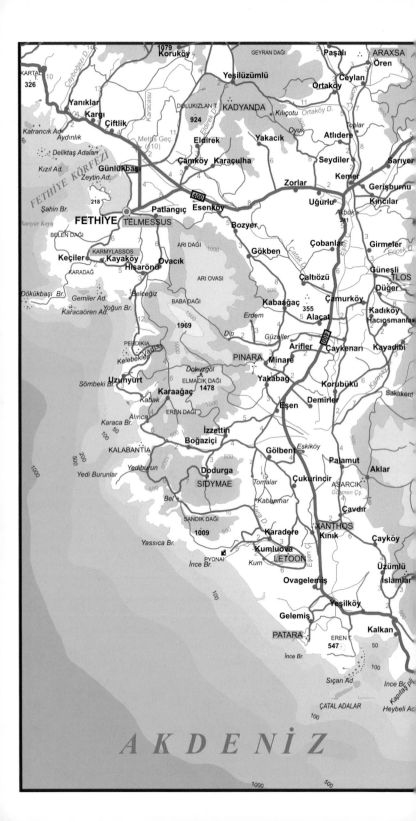

FETHİYE TELMESSOS

+36° 37′32,60′′ • +29° 7′ 7,18′′

Fethiye, known as Telmessos in the antique period, is the most important city of Lycia - one of the oldest Anatolian civilizations - at the western borderline with Caria. Despite lack of information regarding its establishment, it is stated in the available documents that the history of the city reaches far back to 5th century B.C. A. Lycia legend explains the source of the name  Telmessos as follows: "God Apollon falls in love with the youngest daughter of the King of Finike (Phoenike), Agenor. He disguises himself as a small dog and thus gains love of the shy, withdrawn daughter. They name their son Telmessos". The city, with its name believed to have come from that of Telmessos - Son

Amnytas rock tomb.

View from Fethiye.

of God Apollon -, forms the first state of the Persians after being invaded by the Persian King Harpagos in 547 B.C. along with all other Lycian and Carian cities. Telmessos then joins the Attik - Delos Union established in mid. 5th century B.C. and, although it later leaves the union as an independent city, continues its relations till 4th century B.C.

Museum.

A rumor is that the city, invaded by B. Iskender (Alexander the Great) on his Asian cruise of invasion in the winter of 334-333 B.C. has yielded to him with his own will. Another legend is that: Alexander the Great on a mission to invade Anatolia, enters Telmessos harbor with his fleet. Their Commander Nerkos asks permision of Antipatrides, ruler of the city, for his musicians and slaves to enter the city. On getting the permission, the warriors with guns hidden in the flute boxes capture the acropolis during the feasts held at night".

The city has been handed over to the son of Lysimachos in 240 B.C. by Ptolomy III. By the treaty signed in 189 B.C. after the Magnesia war, the Romans have left the city to Eumenos, the king of Bergama. After the Bergama Kingdom collapses, Telmessos, in 133 B.C., joins the Lycian Federation and is one of the six most important cities of the group. In the 8th century its name is changed as Anastasiopolis to honor the Byzantian Emperor Anastasios II.

Lycian Sarcophagus.

The city, taken over in 1284 by Menteşeoğulları, receives the name MEĞRI, meaning the far city, after its inclusion in Ottoman land in 1424. In 1934, the city has been re-

Theater.

General Appearance.

named as "FETHIYE" to the honor of Fethi Bey, a martyr pilot.

Amyntas king tomb, one of the most splendid examples of the Lycian civizilation, lies noble with its long years, coupled with the grandeur of the mountain whose slope it rests upon, and seems like a volunteering guide to your journey through history. This tomb is in the form of a temple built in Ion style, and has a landing with adjacent pillars at the two sides, with four steps leading to it. In the middle of the letfmost pillar, "Amyntas: son of Hermapias" is engraved in 4th century B.C. letters. At the top there is a head piece with three actoters, one

Sarcophagus.

in ruins, and at the bottom there is a dentile fresco. Three stone benches go along the three walls of the flat-topped tomb chamber, with a door leading into it that has iron nail-like joints carved out of stone at its four corners. Although two of the numerous other tombs at the left of the hill look like the Amyntas tombs, they are much smaller. Within the town and in the vicinity a lot more tombs may be found, some sarcophagus tombs and some cutout pieces of rock. One of the best examples of these sarcophagus tombs is located to the east of the government building. Both sides of its arched, Gothic style lid are decorated with war secenes and the two-storey front face

Sarcophagus.

Fethiye Marina.

has carvings that look like wooden, square joints. At the high Acropolis hill behind the city a mediaeval castle, believed to be the remains of Saint John's knights, catches the eye. There is not much in the castle except some writings carved on the walls and a cistern of unknown origin. The theater is on the west,

close to the city center. Fellows in 1838 found it "in pretty good shape".

The excavations were started in 1994 and restoration work continues in 1996. Another old building in Fethiye that has remained up to this day is an ancient mosque that Cezayirli Hasan Paşa has ordered to be constructed in 1791.

Paragliding in Dead Sea (Ölü Deniz).

An ancient peculiarity of the city is that it has been famous for its soothsayers. It is known that soothsayers of this city that has been devoted to God Apollon have had great impact on the course of history.

ÖLÜDENİZ

+36° 32′58,14″ • +29° 6′ 40,53″

The Ölüdeniz Kumburnu Park and the Belcekız Beach, the favourites of the world tourism, at a distance of 15 km to the city center of Fethiye, are situated at the foot of Babadağ, which deserves to be part of the world heritage eith its rich flora and convenience for paragliding.

(Kayaköy) Rock Village.

KAYA VILLAGE

+36° 34´31,89´´ • +29° 5´ 32,01´´

Kaya was a fascinating settlement where the Anatolian Greeks lived until 1922 and was named as "Levissi". As a result of an agreement signed by the two countries in 1922 for population Exchange, the Turks in Thrace and the Greeks in Anatolia were asked to the local conditions and vacated the area in ashort while.

Sarcophagus.

GEMİLER CAVE

The St. Nicholas Island is located near Ölüdeniz. Santa Claus, the Saint of Sailors, is believed to have lived here, and tha island is famed by the church constructed in his honour during the 4th century. You can reach the Gemiler Bay by a 2,5 km. road from Kaya Village and take a boat from there to the island to see the ruins from the Byzanthian times. Furthermore, daily boat tours are organized to the island and the other coves from Ölüdeniz during summer months.

Ships from bay views.

SAKLIKENT CANYON

+36° 28´ 24,65´´ • +29° 24´ 14,15´´

High in the mountains above Fethiye, rushing torrents of icy cold water cut a narrow gorge through the mountains over thousands of years, creating Saklıkent Gorge. A natural wonder, the resulting canyon is 300 meters deep and 18 kilometers long and offers visitors one of the most breathtaking excursions in all of Turkey.

Saklıkent Canyon views.

Candianda city ruins.

CANDİANDA ÜZÜMLÜ

+36° 42′ 54,30″ • +29° 14′ 8,42″

Cadianda, whose Lycian name is Cadavanti, is located near the Üzümlü town, 12 miles to Fethiye. This historical city dating back to the 5th century B.C. was a

very colourful and rich settlement during the Roman Empire.

On the northern entrance, surrounded by the city walls built with irregular stones, at an altitude of 1968 feet, there are four Lycian tombs. Three of them, probably built in the 4th century, are house-tombs and are in ruins. The fourth is carved out of a single rock; on its south face there is a figure of a man on horse back attacking his opponent with a spear and a shield. The first buildings seen on the northern entrance to the acropolis are remains of a supposedly Doric temple and ruins of a public bath cut out of stone which was built by the order of Vespasianus, the Roman Emperor.

There is a small theater on the west side, built on the slope, with most of the seats intact, but the stage is in complete ruins.

Üzümlü village Panoroma.

In the center of the town there is a large plain, approximately 30 feet long which is believed to be the city stadium.

Many inscription found in excavations deal with athletic festivals organized and held in Cadianda support this view. Another supporting evidence is pedestals found around the stadium which must have been for statues of successful athletes.

Theater.

ARAXA (ÖREN)

+36° 72′ 23,51″ • +29° 38′ 74,41″

Araxa is located at the upper, northern end of the Xanthian valley, close to the mountains, near the village of Ören. There are several inscriptions with the name of the city.

The ancient geographers named the city. However, until a long decree of the people of Araxa, listing the public services of the prominent citizen, Orthagoras, was found in 1946 at Ören, not much information was available.

The stone was used as a washing board, and the lines of writing provided an admirable surface. On the basis of this decree, we learn that in the second century B.C. Araxa was engaged in wars with Bubon and Cibyra who invaded the territory and enslaved a number of Araxan citizens. Orthagoras was sent as an ambassador to raise the issue with the League. At attempted tyrannies at Tlos and Xanthos, Orthagoras served most satisfactorily in the League army until all uprising was supressed, as well as during the war between the Lycians and Termessus. He aided in the admission of Orloanda, a neighbour of Araxa, to the League and he also served as an ambossador to meet certain Roman envoys. All the time his services were voluntary and he was always successful in his tasks.

There is not much left from Araxa. There are ruins of a massive building in the village. One of the walls stands at a height of 10 feet, made of well-fitted polygonal blocks. On the low acropolis hill, a little below the summit, there are remains of a solid wall and a projecting tower, 18

City remains.

feet long. Many of the blocks have drafted edges. By the riverside there are numerous 'Gothic' sarcophagus lids with illegible inscriptions.

The most significant group of tombs are located to the west of the village, cut in the rock at the base of a low hillock by the roadside. Most of them are Lycian house-type. In one of them the porch is flanked by two antae, each with two rosettes in in the group, but it is not original; it relates to a re-use of the tomb much later, perhaps in Roman times, and the man in question is not to be identified with the Araxan hero.

From Ören towards the mountains there is a very rich spring which immediately forms a deep, strong stream, eventually joining the main course of the Xanthus. There was a local legend in ancient times that

Canyon view from the Cave Church.

front and one on each side; above is an architrave with two fasciae, a dentil freize, a slight cornice, and a naked pediment. Entrance to the main chamber with three chambers is through a tall door. There is also a plain Lycian tomb with the name Orthagoras carved on both sides of the door. This is the only inscription Leto gave birth to Apollo and Artemis not on Delos but in Lycia; the poet writes that the river Xanthus was revealed to men by her, when "in the bitter pangs of her divine labour she tore up with her hands the hard soil of Lycia". An inscription found at Sidyma localizes the birth precisely at Araxa.

Canyon

Cave Church Remains.

Tlos (Kale Asar - Yaka Village)

+36° 33′ 9,31″ • +29° 25′ 15,25″

One of the oldest settlements in the Lycian region, Tlos, is located at 7.4 miles from Kemer. The name of the city appears as TLAWA in Lycian inscriptions and the 14th century B.C. Hitite documents mention it as "DALAWA ON THE LANDS OF LUKKA". The acropolis is on a hill with a steep cliff on the north-east. At the summit there is a castle from the Ottoman period which overshadows all ruins of earlier dates.

The castle is supposed to be built by Kanlı Ali Ağa (Bloody Chief Ali) who reigned in the region during the 14th century. Below the castle on the eastern slopes there are ruins of walls from the Lycian period, and in the south the city walls are one of the best samples of Roman masonry. On the same hill there are groups of Lycian rock-tombs which meet the eye.

The stadium, with the seats of stone blocks sloping down the hill, is just below the city walls in the south. At the south end of the ruins a little to the east there are remains of a public bath adjoining the Paleasta and Gymnasium. The agora is on the vast square on the east, a 30 feet wide, long building with about half a dozen doors. On the eastern edge of the same square there is a well-peserved theather. Below the northern wall of the theater, the

Roman Bath.

City Remains.

"IZRARA MONUMENT" is located, with parts of the inscriptions legible.

The most significant one of the numerous rock-tombs carved on the face of the acropolis is the

BELLEREPHONTES TOMB where the hero is depicted fighting the three-headed monster Chimera, riding on his winged-horse Pegasus. The wall of the main chamber of this temple-tomb is in three sections, and there are two rectangular columns between the entrance and the pediment.

In the middle there is a decorative door lined with two doors opening into the main chamber. The Side doors are elevated from the floor by 35 inches with blocks where there are reliefs of horse figures at the front, serving as thresholds. At the entrance Bellerophontes is depicted on his horse Pegasus, fighting with Chimera, on. Speaking of Bellerophontes, let us recall one of the oldest and intriguing Lycian legend about this brave warrior:

In Grecian times Bellerophontes, the brave son of the Korintos hero Flaukos, Korintos sees a flying horse. This is Pegasus, born of the

Castle of Bloody father Ali.

Stadium.

blood of Medusa, the only mortal among the gold-winged, bronze-handed gorgos, with snakes woven into her hair. Bellerophontes yearns to possess this horse the moment he sets his eyes on this extraordinary creature.

However, Pegasus is quite wild and very hard to catch. Guided by the city's soothsayer, Bellerophontes pleads with goddess Athena who hands him a golden bridle to tame this divine horse. With this bridle Pegasus immediately becomes tame. From that day on Bellerophontes and Pegasus become inseparable. This famous Greek commander accidentally kills his brother in a hunting session and is forced to leave his country. He arrives at Tirynthe where Anteia, the queen (and also the daughter of the Lycian king) falls in love with this young, handsome warrior, but Bellerophontes refuses her. Anteia then approaches her husband, saying, 'O Proete, either kill yourself or kill this scoundrel who wants to rape me !' The king is furious by the betrayal on the part of his guest but at the same time does not wish to be subjected to gods wreath by killing him, so, instead, sends him to his father-in-law with a letter in where he asks the Lycian king to behead him.

The Lycian king welcomes the warrior on the banks of the Xanthian river and orders a 9 day feast in his honour. On the morning of the tenth day, Bellerophontes hands King lobates the letter from his son-in-law. Upon reading the con-

Roman Bath.

tents, the king symphatizes with his son-in-law but cannot justify killing a guest.

Therefore, he sets Bellerephontes to the task of killing Chimera which terrorizes Lycia.

This lion-headed, snake-tailed monster with the body of a horse, breathes flames and turns everything to ashes. Bellerephontes rides on his winged horse, flies up and thrusts his iron-tipped lead spear into the monster's mouth. Melting iron and lead fills the monster's mouth and kills him lobates, admiring Bellerephontes courage and decency, believes that he is the offspring of gods and lets him get married to his second daughter Fione, also declaring him as his successor to the throne.

Nekropolis.

Theater.

Bellerephontes is so filled with self-admiration that he wants to be settled on Mount Olympus. Zeus is annoyed by such impudence. As Bellerephontes proudly rises up to the skies on Pegasus, a forest fly sent by Zeus bites the horse, causing it to buck and throw off its rider. Bellerephontes crashes down on the rocks and Pegasus soars up to the sky, forming the constellation known by its name.

Izuzu Monument Remains.

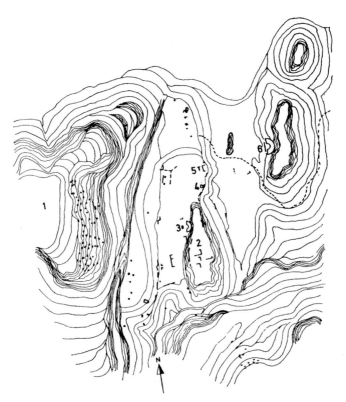

1-Odeon, 2-Temple, 3-Temple, 4-Theater, 5-Roman Rock Tombs.

Acropolis of Pınara.

PINARA · MİNARE

+36° 29′ 26,83′′ · +29° 19′ 30,37′′

George Bean writes as follows: "The Carian poet Panyasis, a kinsman of Herodotus in the fifth century B.C., wrote that Tremiles, who lived by the river Xanthos, fathered four sons, Tlos, Xanthus, Pinarus and Cragus, thus inaugurating the Lycian nation.

This 'eponymous' founder of Pinara is as unsubstantial as the rest. Another story was told by the Xanthian historian Menecrates to the

Sarcophagus.

Theater.

effect that the Xanthians, suffering from overpopulation, 'divided their elders into three groups, one of which went to Mt. Cragus and founded a city on a round peak and called it Pinara, which being enterpreted means 'round'; for the Lycians called all round things Pinara' Whatever credence this story may deserve, the explanation of the name seems likely to any one who has seen the remarkable circular crag which towers above the ruins. In actual fact the Lycian name in inscriptions is not Pinara but Pinale; the interchange of liquids is of course common enough".

There may have been a citizen of Pinara at Troy. Homer mentions a Lycian archer named Pandarus fighting in the Trojan army. Strabo also writes that there was a cult of Pandarus at Pinara. Although historical recordings are insufficient, Pinara was one of the major Lycian cities which is also seconded by Strabo. Stephanus calls her "a very great city". The ruins justify such estimation.

Pinara had 3 votes in the Lycian league. A dozen inscriptions in Lycian language found on the site are all epitaths on rock-tombs, stating only the names of the occupants. The Greek inscriptions do not reveal more. The known coins all date from the second or first century B.C.

When Opramoas distributed his donations among the Lycian cities, Pinara also received 5.000 denari for the restoration of public buildings. The name Pinara lives along with its Turkish accompaniment. The village of Minare is at a distance of half-an-hour to the site. The village is easily accessible by a road branching off from Fethiye - Xanthos highway. At the climb from the village, the great round mass of rock, which is purpoted to have given the name to Pinara, is clearly visible.

The road to this rock, at an altitude of 1.500 feet, was once barred at the top by a triple wall, portions of which are still standing. Actually there was no need for such a wall at the flat, broad, sloping surface the ancient Pinara was founded. Of the city, only cisterns and rock-foundations of houses made of wood and mud-brick have survived to our day.

At the summit, there is a fort surrounded on the south-west with walls and ditches, but the sherds found here are from the medieval

Pınara Necropolis.

Rock Tombs of Pınara.

times. The most significant item is the abundancy of pigeon-hole tombs carved on the vertical east face of the hill. These tombs are connected by two rows of stairs cut into the rock by use of rope ladders hanging from the summit. They evidently date back to the earliest settlements in the vicinity.

The first acropolis is too small and must have become insufficient shortly whereby a second one was buit on a lower hill.

Around the second acropolis the ruins of the city are abundant. The lower city does not have a wall of defense; the old acropolis was a sufficient spot for retreat. In between the two acropolis, large number of unidentifiable ruins and tombs are spread around. Of the sarcophagi, the one at the south-end is enormous, one of the largest in Lycia. The rest of the sarcophagi are built around this in a square. Just to the south of this group there are two house-tombs, cut from the rock, as well as the remains of a Christian church and

a small theater or odeum, all of which are overgrown and in poor condition.

On the east side of the hill, there is a very handsome rock tomb of house-type, which is called the Royal Tomb. On the door-lintel there is a row of reliefs depicting human figures and horses.

Above this a row of square beamends form a dentil frieze; two of which carry masks sculptured at their front ends. Topping this is a pediment with another scene in relief which is much broken. It was thought that the relief on the pediment represented the instruction of a child and the group above the door depicted a group of happy people. The entrance to the tombs is very interesting; on the left and right-hand side walls, representation of four-walled cities meet the eye, all of the four pictures are similar they have gates, towers, houses, tombs, battlements, and three of them have human figures, one of whom seems to be watchman at the gate and the oth-

Rock Tombs of Pınara.

ers standing peacefully. Some observers claimed that these depicted Xanthos and Telmessos but this cannot be.

At any rate, Pinara did not have city walls. In any case these reliefs differ greatly from others representing battle scenes. Despite the absence of an inscription, this single chamber and the size and ornaments of the tomb suggest that it was built for one person who must be royal.

Unfortunately the tomb was destroyed by looters and the shepherds fires. Further south there are elegant

tombs cut on the sides of a high rock.

Bellow the north end of the hill is a level ground which must have been the agora but which has no supporting identification. On the east of the plain there are ruins of a temple, a foundation about 45 by 27 feet and some buildings which could not be identified.

On another low hill about 100 yards to the east, there is a well-preserved main theater. The cavea forms more than a semicircle and is in very good condition, with 27 rows of seats and ten stairways making nine cunnei; there is no diazoma.

The plan of the stage-building is very clear and the walls and pillars are, in part, still standing to a height of 5-6 feet. Two doors are preserved at the south end and still have their lintels in place; both lead into the space between the proscenium wall and the main building, one from parodos, the other from the side of the building. The proscenium wall bends back at each end at an obtuse angle to run parallel with the analemma and thus form a parodos with parallel sides. The theater as a whole is purely Greek and seems never to have been Romanized.

In the extreme south to the site, in the hillside beyond the stream, there are more rock-tombs but they are hard to reach.

The Temple of Love.

SİDYMA - DODURGA

+36° 23′ 59,90″ • +29° 12′ 19,34″

Sidyma is apart from Arsada, the least often visited of the cities of the Xanthos valley. Like Arsada, it really should not be reckoned in the valley, as it is located on Mt. Cragus, at 1.750 feet above sea-level, and quite inaccessible to wheeled traffic. From the main Fethiye-Xanthos road a side-road turns off 6 kilometers south of Kestep (Eşen); this may be followed by a jeep for another 6 kms, after which there is a fairly steep 800 -foot climb of an hour or so by a good, if stony, path. A guide is essential.

The form of the name Sidyma (like Idyma, Didyma and Loryma) is enough evidence of its antiquity.

There is in fact some evidence on the site itself for occupation at least in the early classical period; but the first literary reference is not before the first century B.C., and the bulk of the ruins, and all inscriptions, are of the Roman Imperial age. There exists, however, a silver coin of Lycian League type, apparently of Sydima, which dates probably to the second century B.C. The city continues to be listed by the geographers down to Byzantine times, but only a single incident is recorded of her history. The emperor Marcian (A.D. 450-457), at a time a simple soldier on a campaign against the Persians, fell sick on the way through Lycia and was

Building remains.

House-type tomb.

left behind in Sidyma. There he became friends with two brothers who took him home and nursed him; and one day, when he was recovered, they took him hunting with them.

At midday, hot and tired, they all lay down and slept. One of the brothers, waking before others, was astonished to see that Marcian was sleeping in the sun and that an enormous eagle had settled on him, keeping him in shadow by its outstreched wings. When they were all awake, the brothers asked Marcian what he would do for them if he became emperor and Marcian replied, "In that unlikely event, I will make you Fathers of your city". When he did actually sat on the throne upon the death of Theodosius II, he remembered his promise and, going one better, appointed the brothers to high office in Lycia.

Climbing the path from the east, the first indication of the ancient

Carving of the tomb ceiling.

city is a large number of open pigeonhole tombs cut in the cliff on the left hand. On reaching the top, the ruins of Sidyma are at once in view and a group of tombs of varying designs, quite well pre-

Necropolis.

served, meets the eye. The most interesting is a small pillar-tomb, consisting of a single tall rectangular block set on a rectangular base with the grave chamber at the top missing; the first piece of material evidence for Sidyma's existence in the classical period.

There is also a group of seven tombs some of which are sarcophagi with gable-shaped lids instead of Lycian 'Gothic' shape.

The main site is on a level plain, about a mile long, running northeast and south-west. The village of Dodurga (Asar Mahalle) has changed its position since the last century and is now in the middle of ruins; this naturally led to damage in the city center.

The acropolis hill, in two parts, lies on the north; along its southeast foot there is a stretch of early wall some 400 yards long and still 10-12 feet high in places. It is mostly of regular ashlar but polygonal at the east end. At one point

there is a small gate with a forecourt and flanking tower. This wall is the second piece of material evidence for an early city of Sidyma, founded on the hill above.

Of this early city nothing seems to have survived. The walls, cisterns and sherds are all of the

Theater

Byzantine period. However, a little above the early wall there is a small theater or a building that resembles a theater but in very poor condition. Anything else which may have survived is buried under the earth and stones that have slipped down the hill side. This theater naturally belongs to the later city.

The city center, which is also the village center, lies at the west end to Emperor Claudius (A.D. 41-54), Artemis and other deities.

Between here and the east end of the site are numerous monuments, mostly tombs. The most striking one is a built tomb of temple-type, raised on two steps, and seems originally to have had two columns in antis, though these are no longer in evidence. A large slab of the roof remains in place, decorated on the underside with soffits

Remains of a structure.

of the site. Here there were formerly to be seen remains of a temple and stoa sufficient to permit reconstruction on paper.

The back wall of the stoa is still recognizable, with a public convenience set against it, but not much of the temple can now be made out. It was quite small, about 30 feet in length, with steps and four columns on the west front and was dedicated "to the Savior Gods the Emperors".

Part of the inscription of the stoa was also found, with a dedication containing human heads and rosettes in relief. The heads are beardless and appear to be female. At the rear a plain opening leads to a lower chamber.

Close by is a row of sarcophagi, two of which especially catch the eye. Their form is identical and they rest on a common base. They have a gable-shaped roof with acroteria at the lower corners. The badly weathered inscriptions indicate that they belong to a father and son, bearing the same name, Aristodemis.

One inscription reveals that the occupant is a court physician honoured by the emperors; the other is in verse, the initial letters of the lines forming an acrostic, Aristodemus.

At a short distance to the southwest there is a 30 foot high building, resting on a low substructure which originally was the base of a large built tomb. The building is of a much later date, with earlier, inscribed blocks re-used. There are windows high up in the walls. The door on the north is decorated with lions heads on the lintel and a rosette at the top of each jamb. A low door in the real wall of the substructure lead to the basement of the original tomb. There is also another building further to the west which might have been baths, but only two arches are left standing side by side.

In the village a mosque has been constructed, largely out of the stones of Sidyma; let into its back

(an ancient inscription in the upper wall) Village Mosque.

wall is an unusual inscription headed "The Gods here", followed by a list of twelve deities.

The names are all familiar, Zeus, Apollo, Artemis, Athena, Aphrodite, and so forth, but amazingly, two deities named in other inscriptions, Hecate and Serapis, are not included. The Twelve Gods of Lycia are well known, but they are anonymous; was the present list perhaps restricted to twelve in order to give them names? It is not to be supposed that all twelve possessed temples at Sidyma; in fact the only temple yet identified on the site is dedicated to the Emperors.

Necropolis hill.

LETOON

+36° 19′ 53,76′′ • +29° 17′ 19,29′′

Across the river from Xanthus, 2.5 miles to the south-west and 2 miles from the coast is the well-known sanctuary of Leto. Until 1962 little was to be seen beyond a theater and a mass of blocks marking the site of a temple; since then the French excavators have uncovered the major part of the sanctuary and adjoining buildings, working largely under the water - table, and have recovered many interesting documents concerning it.

According to the history of antiquity, Hera was filled with disgust when Zeus fell in love with Leto. Persecuted by a jealous and unforgiving wife, Leto wandered around and finally arrived at Delos. Here she gave birth to Apollon and Artemis. In all the countries she visited, including Lycia, there are various stories about Leto. Once, when she came near a fountain to quench her thirst, she was driven away by the shepherds. After the children were born, Leto returned to Lycia and punished the shepherds by turning them into frogs. In another story, Leto, aided by wolfes, arrives at the river of Xanthos and quenches her thirst. In memory of this occasion she changed the name of the country from Termilis to Lycia. It is also said that Apollon and Artemis were born in Lycia. In another story, Lito befriends an old woman named Syssa and stays at her cottage.

Some claim that the cult of Leto existed in Lycia prior to the Greek period and her name may be related to LADA which in Lycian language means "woman" or "wife". There are other shrines of Leto in Calinda and

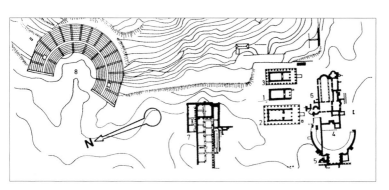

1-Artemis Tempel, 2-Leto Temple, 3-Apollon Temple, 4- The memorial fountain, 5-Exedra, 6- Monastery 7- Portico 8- Theater.

Psychus in the north-west but none of them are so famous as the one at Xanthos. Leto and her children are national heroes of Lycia and Letoon was the federal sanctuary of the Lycian League.

National festivals were organized here. The priests were the chief priests of the League. The ruins brought to day-light in excavations confirm the size and prominence of this sanctuary.

Temple remains.

In the center of the ruins are three temples, with nothing much in evidence above floor-level. In the east, by the rocky ledge, there is a Doric temple with a peristyle of eleven columns on the sides and six at the ends which dates back to the second century B.C.

It has a pronaos, a cella and an opisthodomos and the walls of the cella are decorated with half-engaged columns. At the west end, is a larg-

Leto temple.

er temple, Ionic in style, built at an earlier date. Here the ruins are better preserved and may be restored. This too has a peristyle of eleven colums by six and half-engaged columns in the cella. There is a third, smaller temple between these two, with a rocky outcrop on the north. In this temple there is an inscription in Lycian language, dating to the 5th or 4th century, dedicated to Artemis (ERTEMIT). Although there is no definite evidence regarding the other two temples, it is assumed that they are built for Leto and Apollo respectively.

Excavations in the southern and western regions of the main temple (Apollo ?) revealed a large nymphaeum connected with the sacred spring.

A rectangular building, situated in west-east direction, is surrounded by a large, semi-circular paved basin and on the north there are two semi-circular exedrae. This was built in the 3rd century A.D. and is located over a Hellenistic building constructed at an earlier date. Excavations are carried out mostly below water level.

Theater.

Leto Apollo and Artemis Temples.

On part of the nymphaeum a church was built in around the sixth century.

Excavations are presently under way on the Hellenistic stoa and other buildings in the north and west of the temples. The Lycian ruins are on lower layers, but the sherds found date as for back as the 8th century B.C.

In the northern part of the site there is a Hellenistic theater. The seats facing north-west are in the shape of more than a semi-circle. The theater is cut out of the hill-side and are built with regular shaped, smoth, rectan-

Theater and temple appearance.

Apollo Temple Ground Mosaic.

gular blocks. There is a diazoma. From the seating rows, a covered passage leads out at both ends. On the inner walls at south-west, there are sixteen masks representing Dionysus, Silenus, a satyr, a girl and a comic old woman. There is no sign of a stage-building. Close to the entrance on the north-east there is a handsome tomb. Half-buried, the narrow door is or namented at top corners with leaf decorations. The interior is quite large, made of beautifully cut square blocks. Between this tomb and the theater there is a polygonal wall of an earlier period, stretching 30 feet and with a height of 5 feet.

Among the inscriptions recovered, the most significant is the one

Theater.

written in three languages; Lycian, Greek and Aramaic. This was discovered on the rocky plain in the east of the temples. In this trilingual text a cult is mentioned which is loyal to Basileus, the king of Caunus. The mythical founder of this kingdom is Caunos, son of Miletus, and his cult reigned Caunus until the Roman times. In the 4th century B.C. during the deity of Pixodarus, the brother and successor of Mausolus, this cult was the major force.

In the inscription those not observing monthly and yearly sacrifices and rites would be judged and found guilty by Leto, her children and the Nymphs.

According to Strabo, Leto is at a distance of 10 stade from the mouth of the river and 60 stades from Xanthos. The first figure may be correct because the shoreline deviated since antiquity. The distance of 60 stades from Xanthos, on the other hand, must be a miscalculation.

We made our hourses graves
And our graves are home to us
Our hourses burned down
And our graves were looted
We climbed to the summits
We went deep into the earth
We were drenched in water
They came and got us
They burned and destroyed us
They plundered us
And we,
For the sake of our mothers,
Our women,
And for the sake of our dead,
And we,
In the name of our honour
And our freedom,
We the people of this land,
Who sought mass suicide,
We left a fire behind us,
Never to die out...

Inscription.

XANTHOS-KINIK

+36° 21′ 24,30′′ • +29° 19′ 7,17′′

This poem, found on a tablet in the Xanthos excavations and translated by Azra Erhat, thus tells us about the Xanthians, who, despite the numerous invasions throughout their history, clung to their Lycian characteristics even at the cost of their lives.

The name of Xanthos, the largest and most prominent city of the Lycian civilization, is an integral part of the history of Lycia. Situated at Kınık village on the highway between Fethiye and Kaş, this noble city, famed for rebelling against tyrannical invaders and plunderers over centuries, was rendered helpless in the face of historical looting of sir Charles Fellows in 1838 on behalf of the British Museum.

Notwith standing hundreds of articles belonging to such a splendid civ-

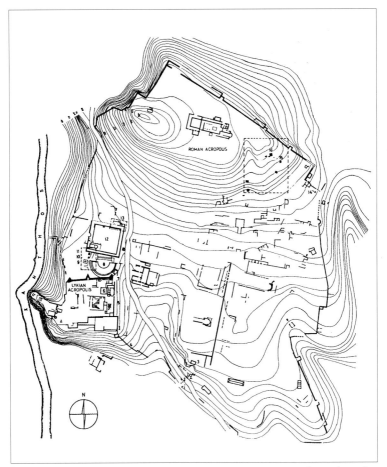

1- City gate, 2-Vespasian gate, 3- Nereid monument, 4-Hellenistic Wall, 5-Polygonal walls, 6-Byzantine Church, 7-Lycian tomb tower, 8-Theater, 9-Roman tomb, 10- Lycian tomb tower, 11- Harpy Monument, 12-Agora, 13- Xanthos Monument Inscription, 14- Sarcophagus, 15- Pavaya monument, 16- Tower tomb.

ilization brutally removed from the site and shipped, miles away from where they belong, to England, the remaining pieces are still most beautifully representantive of the Lycian civilization. The first account of Xanthos in history is rendered in the invasion of Western Asia Minor by the Persian commander Harpagos in 540 B.C. The commander came to the valley of Xanthos from Caria and met with great resistance on the part of Ly-

cians. Despite the superior force of the enemy blockading the city, the Xanthians gathered their wives, children, slaves and household goods at the acropolis and set fire to them, fighting until not one living soul was left. About 80 families, who happened to be elsewhere during the fight, rebuit

the city once again. Following the Persian dynast, Alexander the Great took over Xanthos in 309 B.C. The city passed on to Ptolemy dynasty and later fell under the rule of Antiochus the Third, the king of Syria.

The northern door of the city bears an inscription which states "The Great

Theater.

King Antiochus dedicates the city to Leto, Apollon and Artemis" which indicates that Antiochus, realizing that Xanthos cannot be taken by force, chose reconciliation with the Xanthians.

Shortly afterwards, during the Rhodian rule, the city was surrounded by Brutus in 42 B.C. who sought financial and military aid in his fight with Marcus Antonius. After days of strenuous fighting, the city dwellers, realizing that their resistance was at an end, once again attempted to perform a mass suicide, preferring death to surrender. When the city falls, Brutush witnesses the body of a woman hanging by the

Harpy Monument.

neck, holding her dead baby in her arms and a torch with which she set fire to her house. Eyes brimming with tears, Brutus orders his soldiers to search for Xanthians who may still be alive, offering large prizes for such findings. Only 150 Xanthians could be captured alive.

Supported by the Lycian dynasty, Xanthos is able to revive and once again becomes the most famous Lycian city.

During the Byzantian period, the Vespasian arch, a new theater and an agora are constructed and Xanthos becomes the center of bishopry. During the Arab invation the city lost its prominence in the seventh century.

Byzantine church.

At the entrance to the city on the left there is the city door of the Hellenistic style above which is the arch built in honour of Emperor Vespasia. The remains on the right-hand side of the road are the podium of the famous Nereid monument which is now in the British Museum. The Lycian acropolis is located on the south of the Roman theater. The acropolis, built in the 5th century B.C., is surrounded by a wall formed by polygonal stones put together. The north face of the wall is from the Byzantine times and on the north-east there is a memorial tomb 13 feet high. A large monastery and a church leaning against the wall are the other remains around the acropolis. To

Inscription.

Xanthos Monument Inscription.

The height of the famous Harpy monument on the north, along with its burial chamber and the lid, is 18 feet. When the tomb was first discovered, the busts of winged women on the northern and southern faces were thought to be Harpies but later it was ascertained that these were sirens conveying the souls of the dead to the gods. A little to the south of the Harpy monument is the Lycian memorial tomb sitting on a high pedestal, built in the 3rd century B.C. This is a pillar-tomb and is not a single rock but consists of pieces put on top of each other so as to leave space on the inside. Further south is a third tomb, probably built prior to imperial period, in the form of a tower with a burial chamber. Just behind the Roman agora, on the north, is the famous Panthian Stele. This monument has a pillar-tomb which is a significant historical document with inscriptions on all

the west of the theater are two very well preserved Lycian monuments.

The Byzantine church ground mosaic.

Sarcophagus cover reliefs.

four sides. These are known as the major inscriptions in Lycian language with its 250 lines which may be analysed in three parts as to the characteristics of the language. The writings starting on the southern face and covering all of the eastern and part of the northern faces are in the familiar Lycian letters. This is followed by 12 lines of satire in Greek. The rest of the northern face and the face on the west are covered with inscriptions in a ceremonial language which is difficult to decipher.

To the east of agora on the large plain, which was the center of the settlement during the Hellenistic and Roman periods, the remains of Pavaya Sarcophagus are eye-catching. The splendid reliefs of this monument are now in the British Museum. Next to the Pavaya Sarcophagus are the foundations of a large Byzantine basilica and a lid decorated with reliefs of lions.

House type tombs.

No doubt you will apreciate that it is impossible to summarize the history of such an enormous civilization in these few pages. In addition to the principal ruins we have attempted to list above, you may visit the British Museum to study the Xanthian ruins exhibited in a vast space.

PATARA (GELEMİŞ)

+36° 15′ 39,15′′ • +29° 18′ 53,42′′

Gelemiş village at a 17-mile distance to Fethiye, has become a major site for stopping over in recent years with hotels, motels, restaurants and night clubs, providing a 2000-bed capacity. Another major attraction of the village is the antique city of the Patara, and the Patara beach is only 0.62 miles to the village. Patara has one of the most beautiful beaches in the province, with a shallow sea and a sandy shore 13 miles long.

The antique name of this most significant and old city on the Lycian coast is Patara. This city, which is located at 9 miles to Xanthos was the major harbour and trade center of its period and it is also a famous sanctuary devoted to God Apollon. Unfortunately, the location of the temple of Apollon, famous for its soothsayers, has not yet been established in the excavations.

When this antique city surrendered to Alexander the Great, the empreror offered the city to the Athenian general Phocion as one of the four tax-paying cities, but the general turned it down. The city played a prominent role as a naval base for Alexander the Great. In 196 B.C.

Antiochos III, the King of Syria took over the city and despite all efforts of Romans and Rhodians, it was ruled by Syria until the Apemka treaty signed in 189 B.C. Following the mass suicide at Xanthos in 42

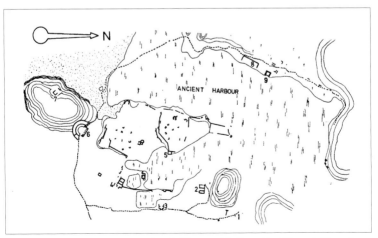

1- Giriş Kapısı, 2- Roma Hamamları, 3- Hıristiyanlık dönemi bazilikası, 4- Vespasian Hamamları, 5- Tapınak, 6- Tiyatro, 7- Tapınak, 8- Hadrian Granariumu, 9- Tapınak.

B.C., Brutus directed his army here and captured the city which did not display serious resistance.

Patara's prominence lasted through the Empiricial period. It held 3 votes in the Lycian League and functioned as the archive administrator of the League. Patara is renowned as the birth place of St. Nicholaus, the priest of Myra. It was an important religious center for Christianity in the fourth century.

Spread over a vast area, most of the archeological remains at Patara are today covered with sand. At the entrance of the city, there are Roman tombs and Lycian sarcophagi, as well as three arches built in typical Ro-

man architecture which are note-worthy.

The inscriptions on both sides of the door indicate that it was built in 100 A.D by Mettius Motestus, the Roman Governor. The public bath built, with donations from the Lycian League in compliance with instructions of Emperor Vespasianus, has five rooms with adjoining doors. The theater built in 142 A.D. on the northern slopes of the large sand-hill is now covered with sand. Further to the north, there is a building, 230 feet long and 79 feet wide, with an inscription, in Latin on the front, revealing that it is a store house built during the reign of Hadrian, which

Monumental City Gate.

Wall Inscription.

Embossed corner piece.

Bath.

has eight chambers in equal sizes. The front facade is divided into two by a recess.

The lower portion are led to the eight rooms by eight rectangular doors. In the upper part there is a window over each door.

Today, in addition to archeological studies at Patara aimed at saving the city submerged in the sand, plantation of trees along the wide coast-line is sped up to prevent the sand layers covering the city.

Theater and the street with column.

Byzantine church.

KALKAN

+35° 29´ 47,13´´ • +29° 24´ 51,11´´

K alkan, located to the southern-most end of the Teke peninsula, by the small bay of the same name, is a new settlement unit. Obviously, the first settlers of the area were the Tekelio¤lu Turkomans who first immigrated to the Gömbe and Elmal› plateaux and, then, moving down to the south, settled and built their villages in the Eşen Valley and the Yeşilköy-Fırnaz plains. Some of the Turkomans who settled in Yeşilköy laid the foundations of today's district of Kalkan which is by the bay on the other side of the hill of the same name in the east of the village. For years, Kalkan remained as a small community annexed to Yeşilköy. In recent years, however, due to the very low rate of humidity of its fine air and the hotel, motel and pension house businesses, fish restaurants, cafeterias and marina, it has become a popular centre for tourism.

Located in the east of Kalkan is the KAPUTAŞ BEACH with its strand measuring 60 m long by 20 m wide between the sheer falez rocks of 25 m height, is the best known natural bay formed by the Taurus mountains running perpendicular to the shore. In the east of the beach is the BLUE CAVE, with a diameter of 60x70 m, having a pebbly strand and formed of sea erosion beneath the falez rocks. The cave is accessible by touristic boats.

Kalkan Marina.

Kalkan Panoroma.

Kaputaş beach.

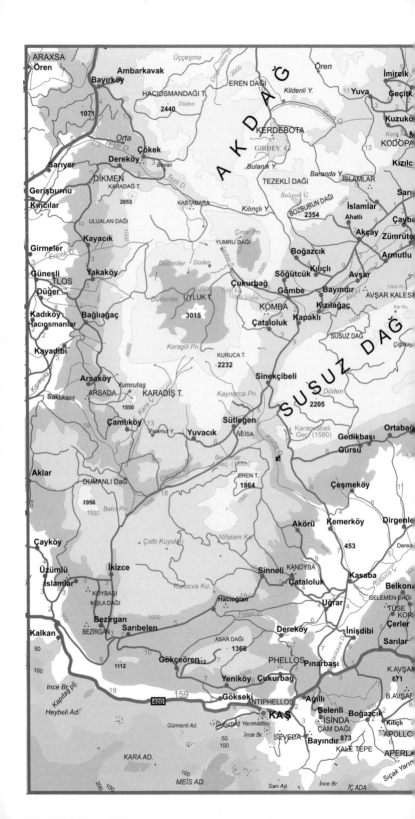

KAŞ - ANTİPHELLOS

+36° 11′ 57,48″ • +29° 38′ 26,86″

K aş was named Habesos or Habesa in the Lycian language. Later it was called Antiphellos. This is one of the earliest settlements in the Lycian region. The rock tombs in the north-east of the city are from the fourth century B.C.

The monument located on the Uzunçarşı street has lion figures and an inscription in Lycian language. The tomb, called the king's tomb by locals, must have belonged to a prominent citizen. It consists of three parts. On the base there are eight lines in Lycian language. The lid contains human figures with lion's heads on each side. In ancient times the ends of the lids were constructed in

Kaş marina and Paragliding.

The inner city streets.

the form of lions or bulls to protect the dead. From the inscriptions on the tombs, it has been established that the history of the city of Habesos dates back to the eigth century B.C.

The figures found on the cubic tomb in necropol are the oldest pieces brought to daylight.

Under the Greek domination the name of the city was changed to An-

General Panorama.

tiphellus. Phellus in Greek means "rocky" and this was the name given to the city in the Felen valley. Immediately opposite Phellus, the ancient name of Kaş, a fishing village, was Antiphellus.

The name must have originated in the fourth century B.C., because in a bilingual inscription found in Kaş, the dead is mentioned as Antiphelit in the Greek portion. At that time Antiphellus was the harbour of Phellus.

In the Hellenistic period circumstances altered. Commercial ties gained importance and Antiphellus grew in significance. During the Roman Empire, Antiphellus was the most prominent city in the region.

The main source of trade must have been lumber from the Lycian forests and the only product men-

Monumental sarcophagus .

tioned is sponges which were found around the walls of Antiphellus.

The harbour of Antiphellus, like that of Kaş, lay on the seaward side of the is thmus. The reefs running out to the sea here provide some protection.

There are no acropolis or city-walls at Antiphellus. There is only a sea-wall running along the shore. Here, regular, bossed, rectangular ashlar of

Hellenistic period have been used. Following the road to the west from the harbour, the remains of a small temple, with only the base in preservation, may be reached.

The road runs to the west where there is the theater. This is small but in very good condition. The wall of the cavea is built with regular ashlar, in some cases with drafted edges, of variable sizes.

Theater.

The 26 rows of seats are still standing. After a short-walk from here, one reaches the rock tomb on the slope. This is known as the Doric tomb with a unique shape. The entrance once had a sliding door.

The interior consists of a single chamber; the bench at the back is decorateod with a frieze of small dancing figures, holding hands, 25 in number.

Among the tombs located on the hill in the north, one has an upper part in Gothic architecture where the inscription in Lycian language has additions in Latin when the tomb was re-used by Claudia Recepta. The tomb at Postane Street has a hyposorium, about 5 feet high, with a sunken floor. Above this is a plain base of about 30 inches high, both parts cut from solid rock.

ISINDA - BELENLI

+36° 11′ 29,58″ • +29° 41′ 38,27″

The village of Ağullu is 8 kms before Kaş, on the Kaş-Demre highway. The village of Belenli is reached by turning in the direction of but before the village of Ağullu. It is 3 kms inland from the main highway.

These villages are at an altitute of 500 meters and they are referred to as the "seaside villages" by the local people. The ones in the north, which are at an higher altitute, are referred to as the "mountain top" villages.

The area is covered by Mediterranean brushwood like mrytle, carob, wild olive and sandalwood. The ruins of the ancient city of Isinda are on a hill 2 kms to the south of the village. The hill where the ruins are commands a view of Kaş and Meis Island.

The acropolis located at a secure site, is surrounded by city walls. Remains of different structures, wells and cisterns are seen inside the city walls. Two house-like mausoleums, constructed on a square podium on a natural rock, are seen near the center of the acropolis. There are inscriptions in Lykian on the frontal of the roofs of these mausoleums.

These inscriptions relate information pertaining to the deceased. The facades of these mausoleums have carvings of four squares inside each other to describe windows and doors. There are numerous Lykian sarcophagi with hipped lids, and rock-cut tombs, also, in the direction of the village of Belenli where the large necropolis of the ancient city is located.

Nekropolis.

City ruins.

Sarcophagus.

THE PHELLOS - FELEN PLATEAU

+36° 14′ 45,52″ • +29° 40′ 1,01″

The village of Ağullu is 10 kms to the east of Kaş, on the Kaş - Demre highway. The dirt road in the western direction leads to the village of Çukurbağ.

Located to the north of Kaş, the village of Çukurbağ is one of the coastal villages in the region which is covered with Mediterranean brushwood.

There are also flat areas that are suitable for agriculture. The village is famous for the almonds grown here. After a 5 minute-walk one reaches the remains of the ancient city of PHELLOS, located 2 kms to the north of the village. Phellos existed in the same time period as the other Lykian cities, and it was represented, together with its sister city Antiphellos, in the Lykian League.

In the years after Christ, when the coastal cities became popular the citizens of Phellos abandoned their city and moved to Antiphellos. The Turkomans century called the site where the ruins of the ancient city are the Fellen Plateau.

Remains of defense towers are seen on the city walls surrounding the acropolis. These city walls were constructed by placing irregular shaped stone blocks on top of each other. The towers, built for defense purposes, were constructed of regular cut stone blocks. Remains of demol-

City ruins.

Lycian house type tombs.

ished stuctures are seen in the east of the city walls.

The necropolis spreads in the valley in the east, and towards the bottom of the hill acrosss the valley. The most prominent sarcophagus in the necropolis is the one with reliefs.

Other sarcophagi and rock-cut tombs are seen scattered in the necropolis.

Nekropolis.

APERLAE - SICAK

+36° 9′ 30,70′′ • +29° 47′ 0,49′′

Aperlae can be reached by motor boat either from Kaş or from Demre and Finike.

Aperlae is undoubtedly an ancient city. Although there are no rock-tombs or Lycian inscriptions on the site, some fifth-century silver coins incribed in Lycian APR or PRL must have been struck in Aperlae. The first mention of the city in literature is by Pliny, followed by the Stadiasmus, Ptolemy and Hierocles. In the Byzantine bishopric listing the name appears as Aprillae. During the Roman Empire, Aperlae headed the sympolity which included Simena, Apollonia and Isinda, and four of them seem to carry one vote in the League. When this was first instigated is not certain.

Apollonia may not have been a member in pre-Roman times. Citizens of the three associates were called on official documents as "Aperlite from Simena" etc. and their own ethnics were not mentioned.

The site is located at the head of a long narrow bay, not on the commercial sea route. It is not habited today. It serves as a landing stage for Sıcak, not frequently in use. The ruins are on the slope facing the sea, on a low hill just above the north side of the bay.

The rectangular land sloping down from the hilltop close to the water is surrounded by the original city-wall, constructed by almost regular ashlar, some parts of which are later repaired with small stones in mortar.

The west wall has 3 gates, in moderately well preservation, and is quite high. Two of the gates are plain, one surmounted by a blind arch. The

Sunken Lycian Saecophagus.

Panoroma of the bay which the city has been.

south wall, in polygonal masonry, has a gate in the middle which presumably represents the entrance to the city and has a tower on each side. Semicircular steps lead to the doorway, which is over 5 feet wide and is surmounted by a massive block, 10 feet long, with sockets for hinges on the underside. There is a large rectangular socket for a bar in the jamb.

To the west of the gate there is a tower in the wall which is in pretty good shape; ten courses of ashlar masonry 3 feet thick are still standing. Within the city-wall there are numerous remains of building, difficult to define due to bushes, except for a small church in the north-west corner and another in the south-east corner next to a chapel.

This area must have been acropolis in ancient times, and the harbour below must have been defenceless. Later, new walls of rubble-and-mortar masonry were constructed, running in east-west directions of the south wall down to the shore. East of these walls there is a new entrance which is now partly in water.

Outside the early wall, in the east, numerous sarcophagi with rounded lid and crest meet the eye. Some stand between the early wall and the shore which indicates that this was part of the later fortified city.

The most interesting discovery at Aperlae in recent times was made by Robert Carter and his wife. According to George Bean, operating from their private yacht, the couple observed and later examined very considerable remains of a quay and associated buildings now lying under water.

From the shoreline to bottom slopes very gradually for about 50 yards to a depth of 6 feet at the actual quayside, where it drops vertically for another 6 feet. Cavering this shelf is a complex of foundations divided by narrow streets or lanes; some of the buildings were quite large, but they are not identifiable. Towards the west end a pier projected outwards, to the east of it lies a long stone pierced with a hole at one end which is likely to have been a mooring-stone. The line of the quay is stepped in, or indented, at frequent intervals, generally of about 50 feet, enough no doubt to accommodate a single ship moored to the quay.

Aparlae, in addition to heading the sympolity, was not a very prominent city and the absence of a theater or recognizable temple is indicative of this.

APOLLONİA - KILINÇLI

+36° 11′ 11,83″ • +29° 45′ 19,31″

Apollonia is not mentioned much in ancient writer's recodings. Stephanus notes an island by this name off the Lycian coast but this should not apply to this city.

Inscriptions found on the site include such references as "Aperlites from Apollonia" and also contain dedications to Augustus and Tiberius by the People of Apollonia.

The latter indicate that Apollonia, besides Aperlae, was an independent city and a minor member of the sympolity. There are coins struck, inscribed APO which must be of Apollonia and could only belong to an independent city. Either the sympolity was not established until the Empirical period or Apollonia was not included in the beginning.

The ruins are located at about 300 feet height above the Sıcak (officially Kılınçlı) village.

There is a road, easily accessible, passing through Sıcak towards Üçağız which reach out to the ruins. On the west the city-walls are well preserved.

There is a small walled area on the summit of the hill, as well as a the-

Building remains.

Antique stairs.

Theater.

ater quite in ruins, a large vaulted reservoir and a number of bell-shaped cisterns.

Numerous tombs, mostly sarcophagi, are located on the north slope.

Also, there are six Lycian pillar-tombs, without inscriptions, and one rock-tomb with a Greek inscription. Apollonia is the city's Greek name and the original Lycian name is not known.

Sarcophagus.

KEKOVA

+36° 17´ 97,31´´ • +29° 86´ 16,98´´

The Kekova road is one of the most picturesque along the Turkish coast. The first village to be reached is Üçağız, which is derived from the Greek word Tristomo, meaning "three mouths".

A channel from the inner part of the bay opens up to the broader outer part known as Ölüdeniz (Dead Sea) and the whole bay is almost closed by the long and narrow Kekova Island. The channel and the two entrances on the east and west of the island make up the three mouths. There are no ruins on the island itself.

On the mainland at the entrance facing the east is Kale köyü, Kekova in ancient times, Simena and at Üçağız ruins of Teimiussa are located.

Remains of the sunken city of Kekova island.

Mills.

Sunken city remains of Kekova island.

At the bay between the two are numerous islets which are flattened down almost to sea-level due to quarries here.

Üçağız can be reached by motorboat from Kaş or Demre, but there is also a road overland. The forestry road opened in 1972 branches off at a point 10 miles from Kaş and passes through Sıcak to reach directly to Üçağız.

TEİMİUSSA - ÜÇAĞIZ

+36° 11´ 51,23´´ • +29° 50´ 53,10´´

Theimiussa is immediately to the east of Üçağız. The name appears in only one inscription as a village.

There are no city walls or ruins of public buildings. At the end of the present village there stands a door whose lambs and lintels are intact and there is a tower or a small fort over a low rocky hill. The rest of the ruins are comprised of tombs.

On the east of the landing-stage there is a pair of house-type tombs with broken doors. Besides the one on the right, a figure of a young man or a boy meets the eye.

The Lycian incription above the door identifies the owner as Kluwanimi.

Further to the east, beyond a small stream, sloping up the shore, numerous sarcophagi present an attractive scene, the larger ones with an exedra in front. Most bear Greek inscriptions with Hellenistic or Roman date, where the owners are identified as citizens of Cyanneae or Myra. The fine for violation of tombs is to be paid to one of these cities. Most of the names are Greek with very few in Lycian language.

At the east end there is a quay or landing-stage, cut out of rock. It is 30 yards long and about 9 yards long and about 9 yards wide.

The rock-walls are cut vertically and the chisel marks can still be noted. The floor is levelled, but the seaward edge is only roughly shaped. There are cuttings in the floor at the east end the purpose of which remains to be discovered.

On the wall at the back there is a gate leading to a sunken road above

General Panorama.

General Panorama.

which on the landward side a tomb is located. The sill of the gate is about 7 feet above the ground.

On the broken sill, the hinge holes and bolt sockets are still in evidence. There is a small opening on the back wall which resembles a window. The lids of the tombs above the gates and at the east end of the quay, reached by steps, are overthrown, lying on the ground.

Sarcophagus with ladder.

SİMENA - KALEKÖY

+36° 11′ 24,35′′ • +29° 51′ 41,38′′

Across the bay, there is the village of Kale, site of Simena, the fourth member of the Aperlite Sympolity. Inscriptions found on the site authenticate its identity. Both the ancient and the modern city are interwoven, overshadowed by a well-preserved medieval castle. The city wall is made of regular ashlar mixed with polygonal blocks and stretches along the southern summit of the hill.

Close to the landing-stage there are ruins of a bath with polygonal masonry, which is fairly preserved. By its dedication we learn that the council and people of Aperlae built the bath in honour of Emperor Titus (A.D. 79-81). Above the shore-line there are two large sarcophagi, one belonging to Mentor, son of Idagrus the other has an exedra in front. Below the castle wall a few blocks built into a late wall and a piece of inscription with the name of Calippus indicate the presence of a stoa attached to a temple.

Within the castle, there stands a charming little theater, entirely cut into rocks, with only seven rows of seats, and a diameter o 50 feet, seating only about 300 people, which shows the city was quite small.

All over the site there are ruins of private houses with polygonal ma-

Simena (Kaleköy).

A view from the castle – Simena.

Nekropolis.

Theater.

sonry, some of which are still inhabited.

Among about two dozen tombs,
two are house-type, the one on the
north with a Lycian inscription,
while the others are sarcophagi, located on the northern summit.

Antique ladder.

ISTLADA - KAPAKLI (HAYITLI)

+36° 13′ 55,63′′ • +29° 52′ 35,80′′

A sign showing the village of Davazlar is seen on the way west, on the Demre-Kaş highway. Four kms towards the sea from this sign is the village of Kapaklı.

The ruins of the ancient city of Istlada are in the small valley next to the village.

Local people call the area, where the remains are, Hayıtlı.

The city is surrounded by walls and resembles a fortress. The main gate is in the middle of the wall that extends in east-west direction. There used to be towers on each side of the gate to defend it.

The foundation of the tower in the west is still visible.

The ancient remains in the acropolis, which is situated on a rocky area, have disappeared completely over the years.

Today, only the water wells and cisterns besides the water canals, carved into the rock to drain rain water, are seen.

The necropolis extends in the east and north of the acropolis. Many house-like rock-cut tombs, sarcophagi, ostotecs and stelles are seen scattered around in the necropolis. One of the house-like tombs has reliefs of doves on the facade and therefore, it is referred to as the "Tomb with Doves".

On the three sides of the tomb, there are blocks of stone placed like acrossbeams. Reliefs of doves and sphinxes are seen on these blocks of stone.

Nekropolis.

Structure remains.

A frieze where the deceased and his relatives are described is seen on the northern section of the tomb.

There are many rock-cut tombs in the western section of the acropolis. These resemble small rooms, and the name of the deceased is incribed in Lykian on the exterior of the rooms. The temple-like mausoleum near these rock-cut tombs is the most famous artifact in Istlada.

In ancient architecture, frontals were triangular and resembled the roof of a temple. The frontal of this mausoleum, however, is round.

Three female figures are seen in the middle of the frontal.

Acroters are decorations placed at the corners and the top of the frontals of temple-like mausoleums to enchance the esthetics.

The decorations seen in this mausoleum are not in the classic style but depict sphinxes and of course, the structure looks magnificent. The decorations in the friezes on the supporting block under the frontal add to the appearance of the structure. An inscription in Lykian has been discovered on the tomb.

Antique ladder.

CYANEAE - YAVİ

+36° 14′ 44,20″ • +29° 48′ 55,74″

Cyaneae is another Lycian city with a Greek name. The word in Greek means "dark blue", defining lapis lazuli, as well as denoting any dark colour such as clouds or the skin of Africans. Since the Lycian name is not known, it is not certain how and why the city is called as such.

Cyaneae is also the name given to Symplegades, the Clashing Rocks, at the northern entrance to the Bosphorus.

Cyaneae is the major city in the region. Although it is mentioned by all later geographers starting with Pliny, no information about the city is forthcoming nor is there any enlightment in inscriptions.

The longest inscription on hand deals with honours bestowed on a citizen named Jason, son of Nicos-

tratus, a contemporary of Opramoas of Rhodiapolis, and like him generous with financial donations to various cities. Sixteen Lycian cities issued honourific decrees for him at different times.

Jason was Lyciarch and at the end of his offical year, when the league assembly wished to honour him,

Theater.

there were objections from Moles and the matter was referred to the emperor, Antoninus Pius, who reviewed the evidence found Moles accusations false, and approved the honourific decrees.

The site is abundantly identified by inscriptions. Many of its citizens are named in various other places, proving its wide influence in the vicinity. Athough most of the remains are from the Roman period, the Lycian

Nekropolis.

rock-tombs and inscriptions prove the antiquity of the city.

The site is located on a steep hill 800 feet above the plain of Yavi. The top of the hill is surrounded on three sides by a wall and the south side is precipitous, needing no wall. The original wall built in bossed ashlar, is visible below the later wall which is in irregular masonry with many re-used blocks.

On the north and west there are 3 gates and the fourth must be at southern end where the ancient road entered the city. Inside, among many buildings, there are a library, a bath, a, large, arched and plasteered reservoir and another depot which may have been for grain rather than water.

There are numerous wells and bell-shaped cisterns all over the site. To the west of acropolis, on a lower summit, the theater is located. It is of moderate size, with a single diazoma and 25 rows of seats still standing.

There are five cunei below the diazoma and nine above. On the fifth and ninth rows of the lower block, as well as on the fifth and tenth of the upper, at intervals of about 10 feet, holes are cut in the floor

Rock tombs.

and in the seats above, which must have held wooden posts for the awning spread over the spectators.

The retaining wall of the cavea is built of small polygonal blocks. Not much is seen of the stage-building. Between the theater and the acropolis there are numerous sarcophagi lining the road which entered the city from this side.

In the west they are plain, with rounded lid and crest while those on the east are varied and some adorned with reliefs.

At Cyaneae, especially on the road coming from Yavi, there is an abundance of sarcophagi, perhaps more so than anywhere else in Lycia. Nearly all are from the Roman period.

Below the city, on southern slope, on the left of the path, the most interesting group of early tombs is located on either side of a passage which may have been part of an ancient road.

The rock is levelled in places and cut into steps. To the south of this, an outcrop of rock is carved into to form a sarcophagus. The lid, of Gothic-arch shape, has a pair of lions heads projecting on either side and there are figures in relief on short ends.

As the lid is in one piece with the body of the sarcophagus, a rectangular opening is cut in the west end for entrance into the tomb. On the northern side of the passage there are a number of rock-tombs, several with Lycian inscriptions.

A tall tomb has the form of a sarcophagus similar to the one across the way, but only one short end has been fashioned, projecting as a facade from the rock behind; like the tomb with ox's horns at Pinara, and

Sarcophagus tombs and city walls.

in fact this one also had at the apex of the lid a similar emblem, not actually shaped into horns but in the form of an upturned semicircle, one-half of which is broken away.

Below the city but well up on the hill side there is another interesting tomb, not easily accessible. It has the form of a temple-tomb in the Ionic order; the porch has a single column between pilasters, with a dentil frieze and pediment above.

The Greek inscription over the door of the main chamber refers to the upper and lower tombs and to the sarcophagus; the lower tomb is in the main chamber itself; by the upper tomb must be meant the deep cutting above the pediment, in which a sarcophagus is resting, a most unusual arrangement. Also, a large rectangular cutting in the rock to the right of the pediment is visible.

The sarcophagus was reserved for the owner, Perpenenis and his wife, while the upper and lower tombs were for relatives.

The inscription further states that the tombs can be opened only by consent of the mindis and that at the opening the mindis must be present to see no impropriety occurs. The date on the tomb is styled in the script of the third century B.C.

TRYSA - GÖLBAŞI

+36° 16′ 5,36′′ • +29° 54′ 1,97′′

There is a narrow pass after the village of Gürses but before the village of Yavi on the Demre-Kaş highway. The dirt road next to the water well on the northern side of the highway that passes through the pass leads to the remains of the acropolis of the ancient city of Trysa. It is only a 15 minute-walk from the well. The remains of the acropolis spread over an area of 500 m in width and commands a view of the Kekova region. As a matter of fact, figures and reliefs of bulls are seen in the friezes and on the lentos of the door of the famous Heroon in the city. It is assumed that these reliefs were removed from the Temple of Adra and placed on the Heroon which is right next to the temple. All these clues indicate the existence of a Bull Cult in the city. The best preserved remains seen today are the city walls, along the southern slope of the acropolis, many sarcophagi and a Heroon which is located in the northeast of the acropolis hill.

The Heroon was built in the Lykian era, and it is surrounded by walls constructed of stone blocks. A sarcophagus, bearing reliefs and an inscription in Lykian, is in the northern corner of the Heroon. Rows of frieze on the 1 meter-wide and 3 meter-tall walls of the structure and the decorated blocks of its architrave have been taken to Vienna. Today, only its cymation (a stone block with a decorative frieze) stands in its

Sarcophagus.

Sarcophagus with bull relief.

eastern corner. Scenes describing events in Anatolian mythology are seen in the double friezes on the inner surface of the walls of the Heroon. On the exterior of the wall on the side where the gate is, fighting Amazons and the campaigns of the holy seven are described in the first frieze. Fighting Centauruses are described in the first frieze on the left of the gate, and a Lykian war scene is described on the right. A death scene is described in the lower frieze on the interior surface of the wall on the left of the gate. A hunting scene is described in the upper frieze. Reliefs of a four horse-pulled wagon and of a Bellerophon are on the inner right side of the gate. Rows of friezes depicting mythologic scenes pertaining to Theseus cover the eastern wall of the Heroon. Descriptions of Centauruses and Perseus are also abduction of Lapits are described, are seen on the northern wall of the structure. At the end of the wall, a hunting seen and Centauruses are described in separate friezes. The seige of a city, Amazons fighting and a war scene are described in the two rows of friezes on the western wall. The entrance to the Heroon is in the east, through a large gate decorated with friezes. On the external surface of the lento of the gate, four bull's protoms and among them a description of a gorgonen are seen. Below the bulls, sitting male figures, and female figures looking at the male figures are described. Maidens are depicted behind the females. It is assumed that the females were the administrators of the city and also the members of the family of the holy priest of Arda. Figures of Bes dancing and playing the flute are seen on the internal surface of the gate's lento. A figure of a dancer, as tall as a regular human being, wearing a cylindrical headgear called polos is seen on each side, on the internal surface of the vertical frame-like block around the gate.

SURA

+36° 14′ 41,73″ • +29° 56′ 38,49″

Sura is on the west of Myra, 1.5 hour walking distance on foot, but it takes very little to reach from the nearest point of the road. The site lies just beyond the mahalle of the same name. It was merely a dependency of Myra, never an independent city, and as such mentioned inconnection with its fish-oracle. At the very end of the plain there is a tiny acropolis, half a mile in length, rising some 30 feet above the ground level, and about a dozen Gothic sarcophagi are scattered around. A house-tomb cut out of rock, with Lycian inscription, stands on the hill and there is a statue-base at the south-west corner with a very long Lycian inscription which is not legible. On the southern corner there is a row of rock-cut stelae with lists of clergy attached to the cult of Apollo Surius.

The most significant piece is the temple and Apollo's oracle. There is a marshy inlet on a steep slope to the

Lycian sarcophagus, and house type tombs.

Apollon temble and church ruins.

west of acropoli, where the temple is located. Carved on its interior walls, there are a number of inscriptions recording devotions paid by suppliants, not to Apollo Surius but to Sozon, Anatolian horse-man god, and Zeus Atabyrius, the Rhodian deity. A Byzantine church, close by, built over the pagan temple, is evidence that the place was a sanction also in the medieval temis.

Pliny records the fich-oracle as follows:

"At Myra in Lycia at the fountain of Apollo whom they call Surius, the fish, summoned three times on the pipe, come to give their augury. If they tear the pieces of meat thrown to them, this is good for the client, if they wave it away with their tails, it is bad."

Plutarch writes that the diviners watched the fish as they would birds of omen, interpreting the outcome according to fixed rules or by commonsense, on the basis of how the fish twisted or turned. The best account is by Polycharmus who mentions a well of sea-water at Surius, saying:

"When they come to the sea, where is the grove of Apollo by the shore, on which is the whirlpool on the sand, the clients present themselves holding two wooden spits on each of which are ten pieces of roast meat. The priest takes his seat

Rock inscriptions.

in silence by the grove, while the client throws the spits into the whirlpool and watches what happens. After the spits are thrown in, the pool fills with sea-water, and a multitude of fish appear as if by magic, and of a size to cause alarm. The prophet announces the species of the fish and the client accordingly receives his answer from the priest. Among smaller fish there appear sometimes whales and saw fish and many strange and unknown kinds".

Artemidorus, in confirmation, records as follows:

"The local people say that a spring of sweet water wells up, and this causes whirlpools in which large fish appear; to these the clients throw their offerings of boiled or roast meat, cakes or bread. The harbour and the place of the oracle are called whirpool".

In these accounts, the oracle is dependent either on the species or the behaviour of the fish. Whales and saw fish aside, sharks are common to the Turkish coasts. The harbour mentioned in the accounts is the marshy inlet, which should be the sea in ancient times; the fountain of Apollo still exists, a spring which flows out of the foot of the hill near the temple, forming a strem running through the marsh to the present coast-line Just in front of the temple, a number of springs well up in the stream which may well be called the whirlpool. The mysterious filling up of the pool may have been controlled by the priest with the aid of some apparatus, controlling the fountain. Between Myra and Sura close to the road at Karabucak, there is a Roman mausoleum, built entirely of masonry and well-preserved, standing at a height of some 40 feet. There is a high and beautifully ornamented door on the north, flanked on the left by a Corinthian pilaster. The interior walls on the east and south have false arches. There is no roof. The benches round the walls inside are in Lycian tradition, and the same is true of the two vaulted hyposoria entered from the back.

ANDRİAKE - (ÇAYAĞZI)

+36° 13′ 34,51′′ • +29° 57′ 18,33′′

Andriake was a harbour town annexed to Myra and it was located where the Demre Creek flows into the sea. The rectangular Granarium with eight rooms is the most prominent remaining structure of the ancient harbour.

The 65 x 30 m structure consists of seven sections and has a big gate in the middle. Next to the gate are the busts of Roman emperor Hadrian and Empress Sabina and they rest on ornamented marble blocks. In the center of the second gate, there are the reliefs of Sarapis and Pluton. Information pertaining to trade and customs is stated in the inscription below the reliefs.

Most of the structures of the ancient city are under the silt. Remains of aqueducts are seen at certain places near the northern entrance to the city. The remains of certain state buildings and houses are in bad condition.

Besides the Lykian type sarcophagi, the remains of two Byzantine churches, the apses of which can be distinguished, are seen in the necropolis in the northwest of the river.

The monumental fountain.

Çayağzı Harbor.

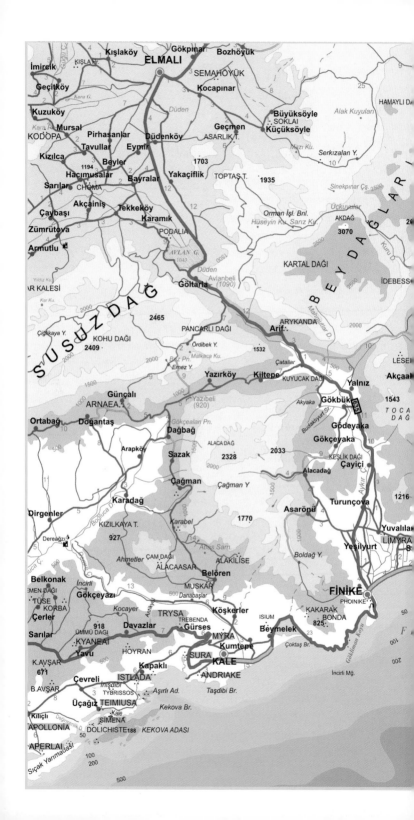

Myra - Demre

+36° 15′ 30,00″ · +29° 59′ 7,10″

Emperor Constantine Porphrogenitus describes the city of Myra as "thrice blessed, myrrh-breathing city of Lycians, where the mighty Nicolaus, servant of God, spouts forth myrrh in accordance with the city's name". Indeed, throughout the Middle Ages, Myra was the center of pilgrimage of St. Nicholas, later called the famous Santa Claus. St. Nicholas lived in the fourth century but Myra was a prominent city before this time as one of the three six-vote members of the Lycian League. Athough its name is not mentioned in inscriptions prior to the first century B.C., the surounding monuments and inscriptions reveal its importance in the fifth century.

Despite Constantine's description the city is not noted for the manufacture of unguents; the only product recorded is rue. After the conquest of

Sarcophagus.

Theater.

Theater Steps.

Xanthos in 42 B.C., Brutus sent commander Lentulus Spinther to collect tax, and when the Myrians rebelled, Spinther forced entry to the harbour, by breaking the chain across Andriace.

The Myrians then had to comply with his demands. The emperors were lenient in their reign. In 18 A.D. the people of Andriace erected statues in honour of Germanicus, adopted son of Tiberius, and his wife Agrippina.

In 60 A.D. St. Paul stopped here on his way to Rome. Opramos of Rhodiapolis and Jason of Cyanea donated gifts of money to the city and Myra became the capital of Lycia under the reign of Theodosius II. Myra was neigbour in the east with Limyra. There was a ferry service between these two cities in Imperial times. At first this was a private enterprise, but o wing to others running unauthorized services, the bid got lower and lower, with a resulting deficit in the city theasury.

Therefore, high penalties were decreed to illegal under takings, even confiscation of ships and tackle. On the other hand, the contracter could sub-let the service on payment to him of a quarter of the fare and the value of the cargo. Passage between Myra and Limyra was by sea, except for pedestrians. The land route was over a steep, rocky mountain. To prevent horses from falling, one either had to push them from behind or give a shoulder to the baggage when passing through narrow straits. The fort on the road and the tombs on the

mentions as being 20 stade away from the sea must be the one behind the theater. Spratt came across a low wall at the summit, fitted with mortar. At the time of Strabo the city must have been on the level ground. Today it is deeply buried and has not yet been excavated. The only remains visible are the theater and the tombs.

The theater is 120 yards is diameter and from Roman times. The vertical rock-face was not suitable for the slope of the cavea and is thus wholly built up. There is only one diazoma in the cavea with 29 rows of seats below it and six above, with 14 stairways, surrounded by two concentric, vaulted galleries, the outer of which is in two storeys. In the western gallery, on the wall between the two corridors, there is an inscription reading "Place of the huckster Gelasius". Here you can al-

heighest point prove the use of this passage in antiquity.

The site of Myra is one mile to the north of the village of Demre, which is a center for growing tomatoes. The Demre stream, called Myrus in ancient times, runs across a narrow valley in the east for 17 miles, before reaching the sea. On the west, 3.5 miles away from the city, lies the harbour of Andriace. The hill Strabo

Theater.

Rock tombs.

most see Gelasius selling peanuts to spectators at the entrance. The diazoma is broad, backed by a 6 - foot wall with painted names, apparently for reserved seats. In the middle there is a projection with steps on both sides leading to seats above. In front of the projection there is a figure of Tyke (Goddess of chance and History), with the inscription "Fortune of the city, be ever victorious, with good luck".

In the orchestra there is an inscription dealing with imports and exports of Myra and the obligation of the city to an annual contribution to the treasury of the League, in the amount of 7000 denarii out of the income incurred from import duty.

The famous rock-tombs in Myra are in two groups. On the steep slope west of the theater there are tombs in various size and types. Most of them are house-tombs. Almost all of them are decorated with coloured reliefs. Some are temple-type but there are no sarcophagi. On the rock-wall of one of the tombs, "Mochus loves Philiste, daughter of Demetrius" is inscribed. On the pediment of the house^type tomb further below, there are two warriors, moving left. The one on the right seems to be grasping the shield of the other, trying to tear it from him. In the middle of the group, about halfway up, there are two tombs, one above the other. Over the upper tomb, in the relief, there is a reclining man, with his wife and three armed men, apparently his sons, beside him. Smaller figures, carrying a bowl and perhaps a double flute approach him from the left. The interiors of the tombs vary greatly in the number and locations of benches, some of which are carved like bedsteads.

The second group of tombs are on the north-east corner of the hill. A little above the ground level there is the monument called the Painted Tomb. This is house-type with a bench on the right and left in the in-

River Nekropolis and Reliefs of the painted tombs

terior. In front is a levelled platform with steps leading up on one side. The most significant feature here is the eleven life-size figures in relief.

On the left-hand side of the porch, a bearded-man raises his wine cup in his right hand to his lips. He must be the head of the family. On the opposite wall, a woman, presumably his wife, sits with her children on either side of her. On the mullion between the two entrances, there was a small, paunchy boy, facing left and holding some-thing like a ladle. A Greek is rumoured to have sawn of this figure to take to Athens, a few hundred years ago. On the smoothed rock-face outside the porch there is the figure of a tall, commanding man, similar to the one inside, dressed in a cloak, with a long staff in his right hand. On the rocks to the while those on the outside show them leaving the house for an outing. The three figures on the extreme right must be a separate scene. It is certain that the family is visiting the tomb; the monument is a symbol of a family dwelling rather than a tomb. Fellows mention colours such as red, blue, yellow and purple but these must have faded in time; only the red and blue are visible behind the reclining man.

Higher up among the group on the east there is a tomb with the pedi-

right there are five more figures: a tall woman, raising her veil, resembling the one inside, with her daughter beside her, holding her hand. Next, round the corner of the rock, a veiled woman, perhaps a servant, is holding out a small box to a young man who extends something to her, may be a flower. The young man stands with his legs crossed, wearing a cloak and pointed cap, leaning on a staff propped under his armpit. Behind him, a smaller figure holds the other's cloak in his right hand. The interpretation of this scene may be confusing, but it is believed that the figures inside represent the in door life of the family ment depicting a lion savaging a bull. In the porch there are 8 figures similar to those on the painted tomb but smaller in size. Here, on either side of the lion's head, there are strange figures resembling dancers.

To the north of these tombs, there is an aqueduct which is an open channel carved in the rock at about 6 feet higher than the ground level. The Demre valley starts near the ruins of a large church and the place is called Dereağzı. The stream runs through a deep valley and is dried up in the summer when it reaches the plain in the south. The aqueduct must have fed the stream and provided water for the city in the antiquity.

St. Nicholas Church

At the western end of Demre the famous church of St. Nicholas is located. Nicholas, born in Patara in 300 A.D., became the bishop of Myra and was later recognized as the patron saint in Greece and Russia. He was also the protector of childern, sailors, merchants and scholars. That he was died in Myra there is certain. He was buried in the church in Myra, but his grave was not left in peace. In April of 1087, a group of bandits from Bari opened the tomb and carrie the bones to Italy. This hindered the Venetians with a similar aim, who claimed that they took the bones on their way to Jerusalem during the First Crausade. The Russian made similar claims. The bones preserved in a casket at Antalya Museum are said to belong to St. Nicholas. The fact is that the Venetians did carry off some holy relics and bones from Myra.

The statue of St. Nicholas in the garden of the church St. Nicholas

The church is not significant except for sanctity and historical interest. An inscription found here states that it was restored by Constantine IX in 1043 A.D., in the last century fan Alstatian group wished to renovate the building with donations from Russia, but this request was refused by the Turkish Goverment. Early in the present century a Russian Consul (a Russian princess) bought the land on which the church stands and wished to establish a pilgrimage on the spot which was also prohibited by the authorities.

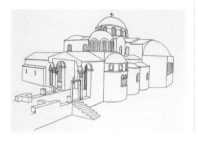

Bones pieces of St. Nicholas (Antalya Museum).

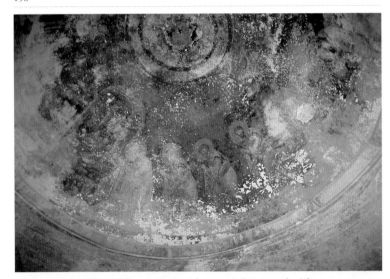

The ceiling of the north east dome, twelve apostles' frescoes.

In the church gallery.

ARYCANDA - ARİF VILLAGE

+36° 30´ 47,45´´ • +30° 3´ 34,97´´

Arycanda is reached by a fifteen-minute walk from Aykırıçay on the Elmalı-Finike road. There are two Lycian rock tombs on the road close to a cascade of ice-cold water falling from high rocks.

Arycandians were pleasure-loving and spend thrift people who were always in debt beyond their means. Therefore, in 197 B.C. when Antiochus fought with Ptolemies to take over Lycia, they sided with him, hoping to be exempted from their financial obligations.

Arycanda was under the Persian rule for a while and then surrendered to Alexander the Great, after which they were taken over by Seleucid and finally by The Rhodians as per the Peace Treaty of Apamea.

In the second century B.C. Arycanda joined the Lycian League and struck its first coins.

Claudius put an end to Lycian independence in 43 B.C. and the region became a part of the Roman Empire.

Starting with 240 B.C. Arycanda struck coins bearing the portrait of Gordianus III. During the Byzantine period the city was re-named as Akalanda and continued its existence until the second century when it was moved further south.

Agora.

The city was influenced by Christianity from the third century onwards.

In a petition found here, sent to Emperor Maximinus, a persecutor of the Christians, it is requested that "illegal and disgusting practices of the godless should be supressed". Later Arycanda was the seat of a bishopric.

The location of the city is reminiscent of Delphi in many respects. It is overshadowed by a rocky region, militarilly defenseless, without a protective wall. The acropolis is at the very foot of the site, just on the right bank of Aykırıçay. Set on a tiny hill, only a ruined tower is still standing.

30 feet above and across the river there is a bath with two rows of three windows and an apse at one end with another window. The theater is small and in Greek style. The cavea is collapsed in the middle, but the seating arrangement is still recognizable on two wings. The retaining wall is in mixed and polygonal masonry and the analemma is made of smooth-faced ashlar. The architectural nature of the stage-building indicates its construction in the second century B.C.

On the slope, the 20 rows of seats are divided into seven sections by six stairs. In the top two seats, there are inscriptions in Greek. Below the theater there is a building with a massive wall of polygonal blocks which is presumed to be gymnasium. Behind the theater is the stadium on a high terrace-wall. Of the seats on the north side, only 4-5 rows are preserved. This is much

Chamber tomb.

shorter than a normal stadium. It was built in the Helenistic period and renovated by The Romans. A short way above the baths there is a small temple, in the Corinthian style, with a pronaos and a cella. The pronaos was later divided into two sections by a long wall.

On the right a piece of an inscription in rough workmanship meets the eye. Beside the left-hand wall there is a Sarcophagus and on the south wall of the pronaos there is an inscription stating "Jesus Christ is victorious". It seems likely that the building was used in Byzantine times as a Christian temple as there are no other churches on the site.

Close to the baths, there are Roman tombs. The largest of these has doors decorated on both sides with a winged figure with a bull's head. The roof is arched on the inside and there are benches on three sides.

On the terrace below the theater there is an odeon. On the southern face of the odeon there is a stoa, 8 meters wide and 75 meters long, with columns decorated with mosaics. The odeon has 3 doors in front and 2 doors at the back, and the seats and walls are in coloured marble. On

Bath.

Tomb in the form of temple.

the three front doors there is a frieze ornamented with masks and symbols of gods, with the portrait of Emperor Hadrian in the middle. The front and back doors of the odeon are connected to the higher and lower terraces with steps.

The Agora is located in the south of the odeon. There are a few shops in the east. The agora is sur-

rounded by a gallery in the south and west. There may have been a temple in the center. The building is semi-circular and resembles those in Tlos. The hot and cold sections are easily discernible and there is a gymnasium opening in the west to the baths.

LİMYRA - ZENGERLER

+36° 20´ 33,96´´ • +30° 10´ 9,38´´

Limyra is one of the most prominent of Lycian cities. This site can be reached by the road leading to Kumluca from Finike-Elmalı. Coming from Antalya, one must branch off towards Turunçova from Kumluca.

Settlement in Limyra started in the fifth centuy B.C. Its Lycian name was Zemu (Ri). The city was most prosperous during the fourth century B.C. It is known that in 197 B.C. it was among the cities which surrendered to Antiochus and that Gaius Caesar, grandson of Augustus adopted by him, after an attempt at his life in Armenia, died here, on his way to Rome. The splendid heroum recently discovered in Limyra virtually certainly belongs to Pericles.

The inscriptions reveal that the principal deity of Limyra was Olympian Zeus. Athletic festivals were organized here in his honour and on all coins struct, the famous thunderbolt appears.

During the Byzantine times Limyra was a center of bishopry but the town was evacuated due to Arab invasions during the 6th, 7th and 8th centuries.

Limyra is located on the south slope of the Tocak mountain. The fortified acropolis is on the summit. On the face of the ridges there are numerous rock-cut tombs. At the foot of the hill,

General Panaroma.

Kenotap of Gaius Ceasar.

close to the road, there is the small theater, in fair condition, with disproportionately large orchestra. The cavea has a single diazoma below which there are 16 rows of seats, with more above.

The remains of the wall is in bossed masonry. The diazoma is backed by a wall of 5 feet high, behind which a covered passage runs all around the cavea, with openings to the diazoma. On either side of the orchestra is a large, vaulted entrance, but of the stage - building only some shapeless lumps and a few carved blocks remain. The date of the building is around 140 B.C. and Liymra received from Opramoas 20.000 dinarii for the construction.

Apart from the theater little remains of the city itself. The acropolis carries some relics of a ring-wall with recognizable gates, but nothing has survived in the interior beyond a few rock-cuttings. Trial trenches, on the other hand, indicate the possibility of settlement here in the fourth century B.C. On the plain there are ruins of several massive buildings, and an old Turkish convent Beside the river, presumably Limyrus. the main feature in Limyra is the tombs, several hundred in number, and collected in six main groups, continuing far to the east of the city. Most of them are Lycian house-type.

Some are plain while the others with handsome reliefs are similar to those in Myra. There are also several sarcophagi. In the western part of the city a tower-type tomb, now submerged in water, has ornamentation in the style of Augustus.

This must have been erected to symbolize the achievements of Gaius Caesar. The most interesting building in the region is the mausoleum at the west end.

Theater.

This monument has been partially restored by Professor J. Borchard. It stands on a large terrace above which an 18 - inch high wall was constructed.

The mausoleum is in two parts; the lower grave-chamber is in the form of a temple in the style called "amphiprostyle", that is a row of columns at front and back only. As an early example of this style, the building is rather roughly constructed. On the several stone blocks of frieze, the hero is shown mounting

Eastern necropolis.

The memorial fountain.

House-type tomb.

his horse, followed by his armed forces, some on foot, some on horseback. Both Greek and Persian influence is evident in figures.

The central acroterium of the pediment represent Perseus and Gorgon. Persians claimed to be descendants of Argive and Perseus. Other remains worth seeing are the inscription on the base of the tomb of Xanta Buras from the fourth century, located behind the theater, as well as the ornaments on the face of the tomb.

The memorial fountain.

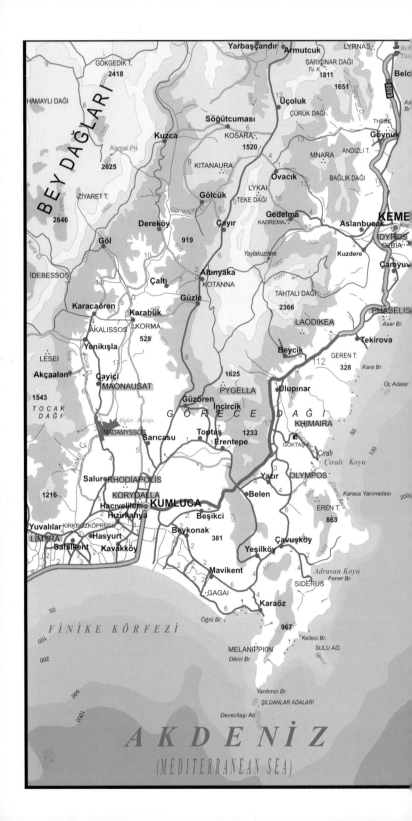

OLYMPOS (ÇIRALI - YANARTAŞ)

+36° 23′ 47,29′′ · +30° 28′ 30,06′′

It is now quite easy to reach Olympus from the highway from Antalya to Kumluca and Finike. Coming from Antalya, at Ulupınar the road branches off to south-east. Strabo reports that Olympus was one of the six major cities with a vote of 3 each in the Lycian league. The city was most properous during the second century B.C. Silver League coins struck in 178-168 B.C. were found in the region.

This site was a pirates cove during the first century B.C. The Romans attempted to banish the pirates from here in 78 B.C. but meanwhile the city was greatly damaged and fell under the deity. The site has been a major source of myths and ledgends of the cult of Hephaistos. A few kilometers away from the ruins there is a spring of methane gas. This natural gas has been burning continuosly since the pre-historic times. Homeros tells of this phenomenon in his Ilyada as follows:

"Hippondes, son of the Lycian commander Glaucos, kills his brother Belleros accidentally during a hunting party. From that day on he is called Bellerophontes meaning 'eater of Belleros'. Heart-sick and penitent, the young man takes refuge with Proetus, king of Argos. Queen Anteia (or Stenebbe) falls in love with this handsome warrior and opens her heart to him. However,

Olympos Beach.

Sarcophagus of Eudemos.

Bellerophontes shies away from offending the king. The queen, full of wreath, tells the king that Bellerophontes tried to take liberties with her. King Proetus is most upset but also fears the wreath of gods in case he fails in hospitality, abstains from killing the young man. Instead he asks lobates, the king of Lycia who is related to him, to take care of Bellerophontes. The Lycian king takes pity on this young and hand-

Temple.

some warrior and finds another means of getting rid of him. He asks Bellerophontes to fight with a monster called Chimaera which is lion-headed, with a body of a goat and a tail of a snake, breathing fire. Bellerophontes, with the aid of his winged horse, Pegasus, fights with the monster and kills him".

The legendary burning stone must be the inextinguishable fire near Olympus.

The city of Olympus lost its prominence during the period of Rhodian, Venetian and Genoese knights and the site was abandoned when the Ottoman Empire dominated the region during the fifteenth century. Some of the ruins are located on the two banks of the delta of a small stream on the shoreline. There is an old bridge over the stream. The rest of the ruins are on a rocky plain about 50 meters over the ground level. The acqueduet crosses the whole city. Near the

tombs on the south, there is a theater and a very old bath. Olympus is also famous for the production of good quality saffron. Close to the south-east shore of a lake in the north-west, there is a handsome door, some 16 feet high, with decorated lintel and uprights, at the foot of which is an

Burial chamber.

Bath.

Harbor monumental lahti.

inscription dedicated to Marcus Aurelius who governed the country in 172-175. The grooves in the doorways indicate that the lids were closed by a spring-system. On the tombs at the west end have letter-oracles. These are in 24 lines, each starting with a different letter and offer two alternatives : "Go ahead" or "wait".

In another inscription, it is decreed that the fine for violation of the tombs is payable to the chief of Police. This was a Roman officer sent to Olympus to maintain peace in the

Water channel.

region. The rock, which gave rise to the local name of Deliktaş to Olympus, is at the mouth of the river, with a natural tunnel about a man's height.

PHASELIS - TEKIROVA

+36° 31´ 24,87´´ • +30° 33´ 8,05´´

Along the road on the shore towards Antalya, 35 kms before the city, the crossing sign to Phaselis is located. At the Beldibi cave in the region, some prehistoric remains are in evidence, but the founding date of Phaselis is established to be the seventh century B.C. Some sources claim that the city was founded in 690 B.C. by Rhodians during the reign of Lacius, while others state that the founder is Mopsos. The latter may have renovated the city. Thus the city must first be part of Pamphylia and later be joined to Lycia. The foundation legend says that Lacius and his party met a shepherd and, since money had not yet been invented, offered him a choice between corn or dried fish. The shep-

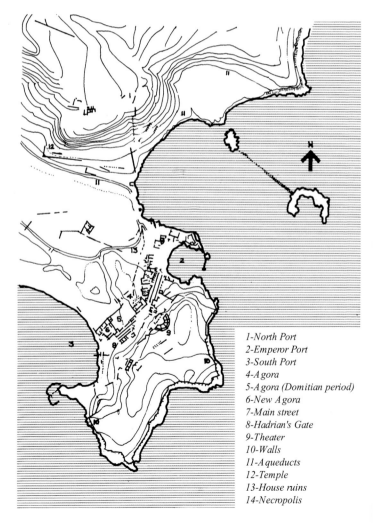

1-North Port
2-Emperor Port
3-South Port
4-Agora
5-Agora (Domitian period)
6-New Agora
7-Main street
8-Hadrian's Gate
9-Theater
10-Walls
11-Aqueducts
12-Temple
13-House ruins
14-Necropolis

General panaroma.

herd chose the fish. Thus it became traditional to offer gods dried fish. Nowadays a small gift is termed "Phaselitian type". The city is on the trade-route between Greece and Syria and Palestine and boasts of three natural harbours. The Phoenicians made use of these harbours long before the Rhodians.

Phaselis came under the Persian rule in the middle of the sixth century B.C. but was liberated in 469 B.C. by the Athenian Commander Cimon. The Greek citizens did not welcome Cimon and were not willing to rise against their Great King. Cimon's companions prevented the general using force. Instead they threw arrows with enlightening leaflets whereby the Phaselitans agreed to support Greeks against Persians and pay a tribute of 3-6 talents. Considering that Ephesus at that time paid only 6 talents, the affluence of the city is indisputable.

In the fourth century, when Persian rule was restored in Asia Minor a certain Carian named mausolus Owas appointed to the Carian region. The satrap, who was an able and ambitious man, made himself virtualy independent of Persia extending his power not only over Caria but over Lycia as well. The Lycians, always jealous of their freedom , resisted, but Phaselis supported M a u s o l u s . Charimenes of Miletus took refuge from Pericles when the dynast's ships blockaded the sea route, disguishing himself in a wig, escaped on foot. In a treaty found in Antalya in 1874, where peace conditions between Mausolus and Phaselis are stated? both parties undertake certain payments and have signed the treaty as equals. Alexander the Great arrived at Phaselis early in 333 B.C. The Phaselitans gave him a friendly welcome and a golden crown, surrendering the city. Alexander stayed

Commercial port.

in the city for a while and lent his troops to suppress the invasions of Pisidians who were raiding the farmlands. Arrian writes that while Alexander started for Perge, with the aid of the north wind, he was able to move along the shore. Following the death of Alexander, Phaselis was un-der the rule of Egyptian Pharaoh, Ptolemy I in the years 209-197 B.C., During the Magnesia wars, the city was part of the Lycian League established by the Romans. During the first century B.C., the city was continually invaded by pirates and even fell into the hands of Zenicetes,

Theater.

Aqueducts.

a Cilician pirate. In 42 B.C. Brutus added the city to the Roman Empire again.

In 129 B.C. when Emperor Hadrian came to the region, the Phaselitans erected his statue and organized festivities to welcome him. A fine gateway was built near the southern harbour and a rectangular forum was contsrutted in his honour.

About prominent individuals in Phaselis, not much is known. In 44 B.C. Theodectes, a student of Isocrates, is famed with his riddles. For example "There is one thing in nature whose growth is unlike the others; when it first comes into being it is very large; in the middle of its life very small, then again very large as it approaches extinction". Answer: a shadow. Or: "There are two sisters, the first of whom gives birth to the second, and the second gives birth to the first". The answer is: night and day. A statue of Theodectes stood in Phaselis. One evening, Alexander, during his stay in the city, roaming the streets, not-

ed the statue and took the wreaths from his companions heads and threw them on the statue, there by paying his tribute both to him and his own tutor, philosopher Aristo. The Roman writer Aelian writes in 200 A.D. that Phaselis was plagued by wasps. Wasps have been seen in Phaselis from time to time but not to a degree to abandon the city, as coins

Nekropolis.

were found in Phaselis which were struck in the third century.

Another interesting tradition in Phaselis is the hair-do which people called Sisoe. In the inscriptions, it is described as "Ye shall not round the corners of your heads". This hair-do may be more clarified by statues that may come to light when Phaselis is excavated.

The Greeks farmed these lands and produced olives, daphne and parsley. In Anatolia the "Phaselitan Perfume" is still produced. However, the unguent extracted from lilies is no longer practiced. In times of antiquity the light and fast sailing-boats were called "Phaseli".

The location of the city of Phaselis is definitely established, and is supported by the ruins lying in the north-east of Tekirova village. The inscriptions here mention the name of the city and most of the remains are from the Roman and later period. In the first century Phaselis was under continuous siege of the Cili-

cian pirates to which the Roman commander Servilius put an end. During the Byzantine period high city-walls were built in defence of

Small baths.

Main Street.

Phaselis. In 1158 A.D. Phaselis was captured by the Ottomans and faded into insignificance as Antalya and Alanya harbours became prominent.

The three harbours at Phaselis are in the west, in the north-east and in the southwest, respectively. There is a brakewater between the two small islands near the northern harbour. Ruins of another break-water at the south-eastern harbour also meet the eye. The north-western harbour is the smallest but by far the busiest; protected by a sea-wall. On the Asar peninsula near the acropolis there is a theater with 20 rows of seats. On the main road there is an agora built during the reign of Hadrian. Here the two harbours join. There is an aqueduct running parallel to the main road, and temple and a necropol are on the left of the entrance to the city. The city-walls surround the whole of the Asar peninsula. At the tip of the peninsula there are ruins of a building which may have been a light house and remains of a break-water. The theater has 3 wooden doors of 3 meters high and beside the entrance

Bath ground mosaic.

on both sides there are two windows at a height of 2 meters each. There is also a small door opening on to the stage. The theater is similar to Roman style and the seats, as well as the ornaments resemble those in Myra.

The two temples on the low hill opposite the theater are erected in honour of Athena Polias, the chief saint of Phaselis, and Hestia and Hermes. In the temple of Athena the bronze-tipped spear of Archilles has been discovered. On the northern harbour there are a few tombs of sarcophagi. On the shore there is a tomb decorated with lions heads and a statue of a reclining woman with the head broken.

On the north side of the path there are small partitions which also meet the eye in the east. Further to the west of the southern region there are three buildings which presumably represent the agora.

The inscription found at the northern end reveals that this is the rectangular agora built at the time of Hadrian.

West of this is a basilika-type church. The building in the middle is a wide, open space with rooms on the east and south. On the path, in the east, the arch adjoining the first two rooms is still standing. Thi inscription in the third room mentions the name of Emperor Domitian (81-96 A.D.). The one at the south end of these three agoras is from the Byzantian times.

At the south end of the path on the north there are rooms which are believed to be the baths. At a later date,

Big bath.

a larger bath was added to the rooms on the northern path. A closer inspection of the theater reveals that there are 5 doors at stage level; with 6 small doors at the orchestra. A curving stairway in the south-west, lower on the hill, represents the entrance to the theater from the street.

The theater was built in the second century A.D. and it is not certain whether it replaces an earlier one constructed during the Hellenistic period.

The most interesting discovery made by the German scholars during the excavation is a fortified settlement on the northern hill. It is on the slope above the marsh and is enclosed by a wall of Hellenistic masonry. A tower

and three archery-sites here confirm its military nature. A passage cut in the rock leads to the settlement and immediately to the south-west there is a rock-sanctuary. Here barely traceable walls run to north.

In the south-western portion there is a foundation longer than 60 feet which may be a temple. In the north-east part of the enclosure is the spring which fed the aqueduct. This fortification may have been intended to prevent the approach of an enemy from the marsh and the sea.

Other significant discoveries are the quay wall in the small central harbour, with projecting bollards at intervals and traces of an ancient road to the west of the city. All ruins, except for the northern settlement are from the Roman and Byzantine periods.

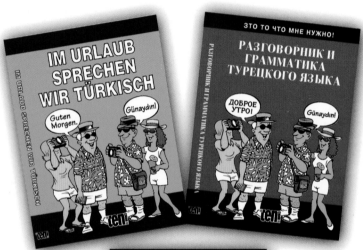
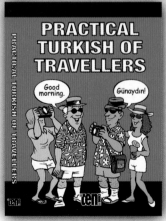